MW00564551

WHERE ARCHITECTS STAY IN EUROPE

LODGINGS
FOR
DESIGN
ENTHUSIASTS

SIBYLLE KRAMER

WHERE ARCHITECTS STAY IN EUROPE

LODGINGS
FOR
DESIGN
ENTHUSIASTS

The Deutsche Nationalbibliothek lists this
publication in the Deutsche Nationalbib-
liografie; detailed bibliographic data are
available on the Internet at http://dnb.dnb.de

ISBN 978-3-03768-232-6
© 2019 by Braun Publishing AG
www.braun-publishing.ch

1st edition 2019

Editor: Sibylle Kramer
Editorial staff and layout:
María Barrera del Amo, Alessia Calabrò
Translation: Cosima Talhouni
Graphic concept: Michaela Prinz, Berlin
Reproduction: Bild1Druck GmbH, Berlin

Contents

Contents

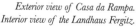
Exterior view of Casa da Rampa.
Interior view of the Landhaus Fergitz.

Preface

Architecture and vacation is a combination that promises relaxation and leisure in a perfectly designed surrounding that fulfills almost every conceivable wish.

Following the success of the first volume "Where Architects Stay" (worldwide), this new volume focusing on Europe is a response to the wishes of readers for an architectural travel guide dedicated to the continent.

"Where Architects Stay in Europe" features 48 new and especially enchanting architectural dwellings across Europe. The hand-picked, usually small accommodations are dream destinations with so many positive qualities that one is tempted never to leave them.

The design of these unique objects is based on their specific locations as they enter into a dialogue with their surroundings. The room composition and the interplay of materials were carefully matched. Each individual lodging tells its guests a unique tale.

The symbiosis of built architecture and charming surroundings invites visitors to enjoy unforgettable vacations apart from mass tourism and away from standard travel destinations and accommodations.

Whether isolated, in a metropolis, near the water, in the mountains or in a city, "Where Architects Stay in Europe" shows the most wonderful locations and lovingly designed and detailed objects across Europe.

Exterior view of the 72 Hour Cabin.
Sunset view from the infinity pool of the Villa C.P.
The ephemeral room from Atelier Lachaert Dhanis.

The range of projects is again very large in this book. Sometimes rural structures receive a modern update like the Landhaus Fergitz by Thomas Kröger Architekten. A former horse stable was turned into a sensitively and expertly crafted country estate. Elsewhere, the mirror-glazed residence ÖÖD house by Jaak Tiik and Andreas Tiik melts into its surroundings, the façade itself turns into a forest that poetically hides its residents from sight, while giving them a full view of the landscape.

But architectural pearls for wellness and overnight stays can also be found in big cities, for example the Harbor Crane in Hamburg, a crane that was converted into a wonderful hideaway with a view of the Elbphilharmonie concert hall, and the Vipp Loft in Copenhagen.

Sleep among tree tops in a tree house or find shelter in a cottage in the mountains of Slovenia, sleep on a houseboat, a historic water tower, or in a bed underneath the stars… Let us take you on a journey of exploration of these small architectural jewels.

INFORMATION. ARCHITECTS>
JAAK TIIK & ANDREAS TIIK // 2017.
CABIN> 18 SQM // 2 GUESTS //
1 BEDROOM // 1 BATHROOM.
ADDRESS> JÕELÄHTME, TALLINN,
ESTONIA.
WWW.OODHOUSE.COM

Sleeping room with floor-to-ceiling windows.
Detail of the shower. Exterior view of the cabin.
Main view from the garden.

ÖÖD

TALLINN, ESTONIA

The idea of the ÖÖD house was born when brothers Andreas and Jaak Tiik were planning a weekend of hiking. They were looking for a small house in a beautiful spot where they could spend the night. However, all they could find were log houses for larger groups of people or small houses of mediocre quality. These were far from the ideal house the brothers were looking for and met neither their expectations nor the goal of the holiday. This experience gave them the idea for an innovative solution, which offers an excellent combination of beautiful nature, accommodation and design.

The underlying architectural idea of the ÖÖD house was to create a design that would blend into the surrounding environment in the best possible manner. This is why the ÖÖD house design is basically simple and harmonious, and does not compete with the surrounding environment. A natural setting is the best location for an ÖÖD house, as it highlights its surroundings whilst remaining invisible itself. The creators of the ÖÖD house say that the more unique the surroundings the more playful the house comes into sight. When the Tiik brothers take clients to view demo-houses, they like seeing people's reactions at the moment they distinguish the house from the surrounding environment.

*Side view of the cabin. View
of the sleeping area.*

View of the chill area. Detail of the bathroom.
Exterior elevation front and floor plan.

GETTING AROUND. THE ÖÖD HOUSE IS LOCATED IN JÕERANNA RESIDENCES, WHICH IS JUST A 20-KILOMETER DRIVE FROM TALLINN (THE CAPITAL OF ESTONIA). JÕERANNA RESIDENCES ARE SURROUNDED BY BEAUTIFUL NATURE AND SITUATED NEXT TO JÄGALA LAKE. ÖÖD IS JUST 15 METERS FROM THE LAKE, ALLOWING GUESTS TO ENJOY THE AREA'S BEAUTIFUL VIEWS AND PURE NATURE. GOING TO SAUNA IS A LOVED RITUAL IN ESTONIA. THE TINY IGLU-SHAPED SAUNA IS DEFINITELY AN EXPERIENCE HARD TO TOP, ESPECIALLY IF ONE DARES TO JUMP INTO THE REFRESHING RIVER JUST A FEW STEPS AWAY.

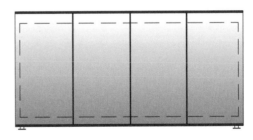

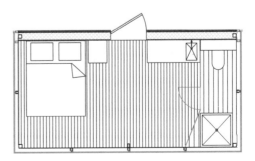

INFORMATION. ARCHITECTS> PAR -
PLATAFORMA DE ARQUITECTURA //
2015. HOUSE> 350 SQM // 18 GUESTS
// 9 BEDROOMS // 12 BATHROOMS.
ADDRESS> QUATRIM DO SUL, OLHÃO,
ALGARVE, PORTUGAL.
WWW.CASAMODESTA.PT

Casa Modesta

ALGARVE, PORTUGAL

The door of Casa Modesta is always open to welcome those who arrive, conveying the feeling they used to feel when they ran into their grandparents' arms when they were little. The project was based on the memory of the current owners' grandfather, an "old sea dog", Joaquim Modesto de Brito, known to all as "the champ". The grandchildren wished to preserve the multitudes of memories that inhabit the walls and grounds. This is how Casa Modesta was born, combining rural tourism with a contemporary feel, manifested in nine rooms with private patios. There is also a garden with a section for organically grown vegetables and a solarium where time flows with the tides.

They built the house from the ground up based on local traditional knowledge, architectural culture, and materials. In the Casa Chã, ancestral legacies were translated into a contemporary language, creating and feeding social and economical dynamics connected to local art and crafts. Cemented in the memory of family and place, PAr consolidated this project by creating a Casa Modesta prototype.

Side view of the house. Dining room with vaulted ceiling. The four matching staircases that lead onto the rooftop. Main view.

Back view of the house. View of the bathroom.
Rooftop plan.

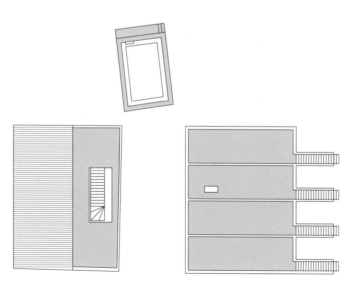

GETTING AROUND. GUESTS CAN EXPERIENCE THE DAILY ROUTINES OF THE ALGARVE SUMMER, FROM GATHERING CLAMS TO BAKING BREAD TO HARVESTING AND DRYING FRUITS. THEY CAN CATCH A RIDE ON A TRADITIONAL BOAT, PRACTICE BIRD WATCHING, SUPPORT THE LOCAL NATURE RESERVE, AND WATCH THE STARS ON THE VERANDAS. IN ADDITION, THEY CAN ENJOY VARIOUS WELLNESS RITUALS, TAKING ADVANTAGE OF THE NATURAL PROPERTIES OF LOCAL OLIVES, ALMONDS, FLEUR DE SEL AND ALGAE. SOME MAY CALL IT A "VACATION", AT THE CASA MODESTA THEY CALL IT "CULTURE".

Living area paved with terracotta blocks.
Sleeping area.

INFORMATION. ARCHITECTS>
MACGABHANN ARCHITECTS // 2017.
HOUSE> 400 SQM // 6 GUESTS //
3 BEDROOMS // 5 BATHROOMS.
ADDRESS> HORN HEAD,
DUNFANAGHY, COUNTY DONEGAL,
IRELAND.
WWW.BREAC.HOUSE

Breac House

COUNTY DONEGAL, IRELAND

Breac House is a modern retreat at the far edge of Ireland. It is situated on the Horn Head Peninsula in the rugged North West coast of Donegal. The site overlooks Sheephaven Bay and boasts an amazing panoramic view of the Derryveagh Mountains with the picturesque village of Dunfanaghy in the foreground. The low-slung linear form is reminiscent of a traditional long farm building and the profile of the roof is inspired by the famous Muckish mountain, which the house faces. This linear design ensures the house is constantly flooded with natural sunlight. Breac House is clad with vertical dark-stained timbers that contrast with the horizontal coastal landscape. Each room has its own spectacular view over the wild Atlantic coast; however, the design focuses on the open plan living area. Consisting of an expansive double-height space with generous glazing and a picturesque view of the bay, the dining area is flanked by a semi-transparent library that runs into the living area.

The kitchen is introduced by a subtle change in level and is floored with local Ardara quartzite. The use of local materials and craftsmanship and the space fluidity between inside and out truly connects Breac House with the Donegal landscape.

Panoramic view from the exterior counter.
Dining room. Exterior view of the house.
One of the external terraces.

Night view from the garden. Detail of the boot room. Dining room from above. Cross section. Interior view of the living room.

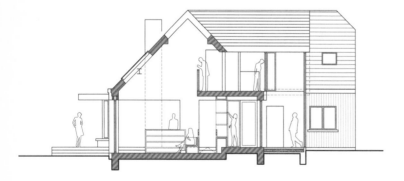

GETTING AROUND. LOCATED ON THE WILD ATLANTIC WAY, HORN HEAD IS A DRAMATIC HEADLAND SURROUNDED BY SEA, CLIFF, BEACH, FOREST AND BAY. THE PENINSULA, PART OF SHEEPHAVEN BAY, IS CLASSIFIED AS A SPECIAL AREA OF CONSERVATION UNDER THE EU HABITATS DIRECTIVE AND A SPECIAL PROTECTION AREA FOR PLANNING AND DEVELOPMENT PURPOSES. LOCAL ACTIVITIES INCLUDE WALKING, SWIMMING, GOLF, FISHING, SURFING, AND BIKING. THE LOCAL VILLAGE OF DUNFANAGHY BOASTS SOME OF IRELAND'S FINEST BEACHES AND HAS A RANGE OF SHOPS, BARS AND RESTAURANTS.

INFORMATION. ARCHITECTS> SNØHETTA // 2017. TREE HOUSE> 100 SQM INCLUDING THE BALCONY NET // 5 GUESTS // 2 BEDROOMS // 2 BATHROOMS. ADDRESS> HARADS, SWEDEN. WWW.TREEHOTEL.SE/EN/ROOMS/THE-7TH-ROOM

Treehotel

HARADS, SWEDEN

Treehotel in Swedish Lapland is proud to present its seventh room. It will be larger, taller and even more spectacular than the others, with levels of experience "in the borderlands between Heaven and Earth". As it is approached from below, its entire underside has been cleverly covered by a life-size photograph of the treetops as they looked before the room was put in place. This means the building disappears from view leaving just the image of the forest as it looked before. The suite itself is located ten meters up in the pines. The way up is an experience in itself. Stairs and landings take visitors closer to the clouds, step by step. When they reach the large Lapland treetops, with views of the Lule River, they have arrived at their destination. Large panoramic windows face north and along with skylights in the bedrooms, they allow guests to watch the magnificent northern lights. The most spectacular experience could well be the suite's unique terrace made of net. A natural pine grows through the net and its branches spread out, allowing visitors to climb out, with the strong net safely below. Guests can either lie face down and gaze at the forest floor or lie looking up at the starry sky.

Interior view of the cabin. Bright living room with fireplace. View from the balcony of the snowy landscape. The Treehotel from below.

The Treehotel at night during the Northern Lights show. Detail of the "new sky", photo image of the existing trees on the bottom of the building. View of the bedroom. Floor plan. Main view of the cabin.

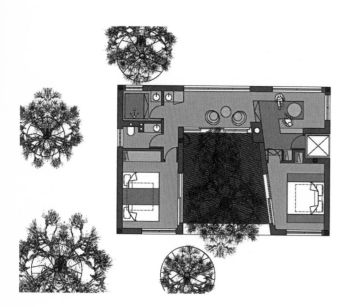

GETTING AROUND. THE TREEHOTEL IS LOCATED IN THE FORESTS SURROUNDING HARADS, IN THE FAR NORTH OF SWEDISH LAPLAND, JUST AN HOUR'S FLIGHT FROM STOCKHOLM. THE SWEDISH LAPLAND FORESTS ARE KEY TO THE HOTEL'S SUCCESS, COMBINED WITH THE DESIGN, NATURAL MATERIALS AND A FAMILIAR, INVITING ATMOSPHERE. HERE, EVEN THE MOST SOUGHT-AFTER CELEBRITIES CAN RELAX, FEEL THE CALM AND JUST BE THEMSELVES. IT IS FREQUENTED BY FAMILIES, COUPLES AND GROUPS LOOKING TO TRY EXCITING OUTDOOR ACTIVITIES, EXPERIENCE THE SNOW AND NORTHERN LIGHTS IN WINTER, OR THE MIDNIGHT SUN IN SUMMER.

INFORMATION. ARCHITECT>
BORIS KAJMAK // 2016. HOUSE>
44 SQM INDOOR SPACE, 24 SQM
OUTDOOR SPACE // 2 GUESTS //
1 BEDROOM // 1 BATHROOM.
ADDRESS> NOVIGRAD, DALMATIA,
CROATIA.
WWW.KUCAFOTOGRAFA.COM

*View of the courtyard. Stone staircase leading to
the apartment. View of the traditional sink in the
bathroom.*

Interior view. Detail of the cube tiles with three-dimensional visual effect around the bath tub. The small house in the Croatian fishing village.

Kuća Fotografa

DALMATIA, CROATIA

Kuća Fotografa, i.e. Photographer's house, is an artistic interpretation of a concept that merges creativity, history, architecture, tourism and social aspects. A ruin that once was the home and studio of photographer Nikica Karavida, who was active between the two World Wars, was renovated based on the local building tradition with a flare of contemporary design by Croatian-born artist Boris Kajmak.

Two elements that determined the shape and sentiment of this house prior to the renovation works were historical analysis of the building itself and the personal story of the photographer and his wife who lived there. Putting those two in relation resulted in the decision to generate a nest-like space for two.

Everything in the house is done by hand by the artist himself.

The house is full of reclaimed materials collected locally and put together in a composition in which the utilities provide esthetics (like exposed water pipes, built-in stone sink, exposed wiring, etc.), with the story and concept determining the space rather than structural elements. The house also includes a courtyard which, while welcoming neighbors, defines the soft transition from the very intimate inner space to a slow opening towards the outside and the small historic town. By definition it is a holiday home but described by many as a home holiday.

View of the building from the courtyard.
Kitchen with traditional furniture.

Dining area. Detail of the pergola. View of the original stone wall.

GETTING AROUND. THE HOUSE IS LOCATED WITHIN THE CENTER OF THE HISTORIC TOWN OF NOVIGRAD, DALMATIA. IT IS SITUATED AT THE END OF A FJORD THAT UNEXPECTEDLY CUTS INTO THE LAND. AWAY FROM THE TOURISTIC ROUTES, IT PROVIDES AN AUTHENTIC DALMATIAN FEEL. PERFECT FOR FAMILIES WITH CHILDREN, IT IS ALSO AN EXCELLENT STARTING POINT FOR EXCURSIONS TO THE NEARBY MOUNTAINS, RIVERS, HISTORICAL TOWNS, AND ISLANDS. SOME OF THE MOST AMAZING NATIONAL PARKS IN CROATIA ARE A SHORT TRIP BY CAR.

INFORMATION. ARCHITECTS>
PEDRO DOMINGOS ARQUITECTOS //
2009. HOUSE> 220 SQM // 6 GUESTS //
3 BEDROOMS // 2 BATHROOMS.
ADDRESS> AGOSTOS, SANTA
BÁRBARA DE NEXE, FARO, PORTUGAL.
WWW.FACEBOOK.COM/
CASAAGOSTOS

*Night view from the garden. The infinity pool by
sunset. The white uneven profile of the house in the
surrounding landscape.*

Exterior view of the building.
Detail of the workplace.

Casa Agostos

FARO, PORTUGAL

The transformative substance of this project originally consisted of a parcel of land (950 square meters) integrated into the agricultural system of Barrocal and a small house in ruins (80 square meters). The ruin displays the characteristics of the vernacular architecture of the Algarve. The strategy consisted of delineating the limits of the central space of the property – a void enclosed by the ruin, the "hedges", and the upland trees. This was followed by the reconstruction of the existing ruin to define the western boundary, the construction of a new wing set back from the existing group, establishment of the northern boundary, and the placement of a water tank on the southern end of the plot. The preexisting house consisting of three interconnected cells contains the guest rooms and their bathrooms. The north wing extends into the ground and articulates the topography with two built patios of similar proportions, one as a northern extension of the kitchen and the other as a western extension of the living room.

The main entrance of the house is through the space that lies between the preexisting house and new wing – a space of transition and fracture between the two wings. The water tank is built to resemble the abundant irrigation tanks of this region; it is a water container with a pure form that emerges from the ground.

View of the entrance. View of the garden and pool from the window. Detail of the white form of the house. View of the sleeping room. Section and floor plan.

GETTING AROUND. NEARBY ARE THE MAGNIFICENT BEACHES OF ALMANCIL AND QUINTA DO LAGO AND THE SMALL BEACHES OF THE FARO ISLANDS. ESTOI, LOULÉ AND FARO HAVE ATTRACTIVE HISTORIC CENTERS. THERE ARE BOAT TRIPS TO RIA FORMOSA AND FROM FARO TO TAVIRA. MEDITERRANEAN GASTRONOMY IS AVAILABLE IN SEVERAL RESTAURANTS IN THE AREA.

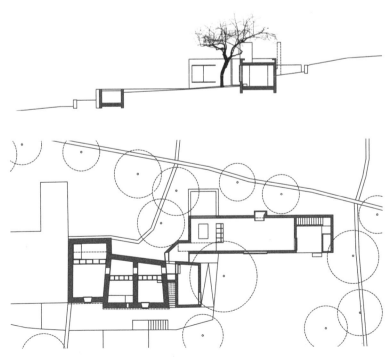

Tinhouse

ISLE OF SKYE, SCOTLAND

Exterior view of the house. The Tinhouse nestled in the surrounding nature. The living room with panoramic windows and fireplace.

Tinhouse is located on the northwestern tip of the Isle of Skye, on a sloping site overlooking the body of water separating the Inner and Outer Hebrides. The project is an essay in landscape, economy, construction and imagination, sharing the same design ethic as its neighboring sister, the Wooden House. While the Wooden House celebrates timber detailing the Tinhouse celebrates corrugated metal sheeting, commonly used on rural agricultural buildings. It does so in a contemporary way by using mill-finished corrugated aluminum as the external cladding for both roof and walls. Inside, its timber boarding, concrete floor and plywood cabinetry give the house a character that is simultaneously modern and rustic. The house was

designed and built by the founders Gill Smith and Alan Dickson, with materials mostly chosen to allow for easy building by a single person. Thus, the handmade Tinhouse celebrates the self-build tradition commonly found in a rural context.

The imaginative use of color also determines the esthetic of the house with highlights inspired by colors found naturally outside: the yellow or pink of wild flowers, the green of grass, the blue of sky and sea and the orange of sunsets.
Similarly, the furniture celebrates the handmade spirit of the house. The completed building marks the end of a five year design and building process and the beginning of a new era as a holiday home.

INFORMATION. ARCHITECTS> RURAL DESIGN // 2016. HOUSE> 75 SQM // 2 GUESTS // 1 BEDROOM // 1 BATHROOM. ADDRESS> ISLE OF SKYE, SCOTLAND. WWW.TINHOUSE.NET

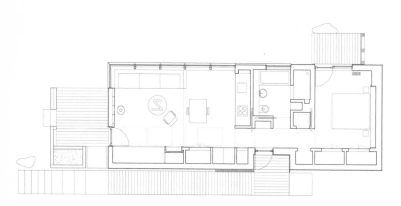

GETTING AROUND. MILOVAIG ON THE ISLE OF SKYE IS A PERFECT GETAWAY. AMAZING HILL AND CLIFF WALKS START AT THE FRONT DOOR, WHILE THE COAST OFFERS PLENTY OF EXPLORING AND FISHING. FAMOUS AND POPULAR RESTAURANTS, SUCH AS THREE CHIMNEYS, LOCHBAY, AND OLD SCHOOL HOUSE AT DUNVEGAN ARE WITHIN EASY REACH. FRESH SEAFOOD CAN BE BOUGHT DIRECTLY FROM THE LOCAL FISHERMEN ON MEANISH PIER, JUST DOWN THE HILL. DOLPHINS AND WHALES ARE OCCASIONAL VISITORS TO THE LOCH, WHILE SEALS AND OTTERS CAN OFTEN BE SEEN.

Night view of the Tinhouse. Floor plan. Detail of the corrugated metal façade.

The colorful sleeping area. Interior view of the bathroom. Side view of the house.

INFORMATION. ARCHITECTS> LOFT KOLASIŃSKI - INTERIOR & FURNITURE DESIGN STUDIO // 2017. APARTMENT> 90 SQM // 6 GUESTS // 2 BEDROOMS // 1 BATHROOM. ADDRESS> MIEDZYZDROJE, POLAND. WWW.LOFT-KOLASINSKI.COM

Interior view from the corridor. Detail of the dining room. Living room with vintage furniture.

Holiday Apartment in Międzyzdroje

MIĘDZYZDROJE, POLAND

The project involved the revitalization and reconstruction of a flat in a small tenement house from 1920 in Międzyzdroje, including the interior design and design of some furniture.

The furniture designed by Loft Kolasiński consists of beds, bedside tables, benches and a table in the bathroom. In addition, unique furniture, lighting and vintage carpets from Poland, the Czech Republic, Denmark and Italy were previously added.

The walls, old floor and windows of the apartment have very interesting structures. After removing the old plaster, half-timbered walls were found in the whole apartment. In the bathroom, one wall was particularly unique as it consisted of a mix of short wooden planks and clay. It was decided to keep the wall's structure visible by covering with just a single layer of paint.

GETTING AROUND. THE APARTMENT IS LOCATED IN MIĘDZYZDROJE, ON THE POLISH COAST WITH EXTENSIVE BEACHES OF SOFT WHITE SAND. IT IS A BEAUTIFUL SMALL CITY WITH OLD VILLAS SURROUNDED BY FOREST. IN SPRING, SUMMER AND AUTUMN IT IS PERFECT FOR LONG WALKS ON THE BEACH.

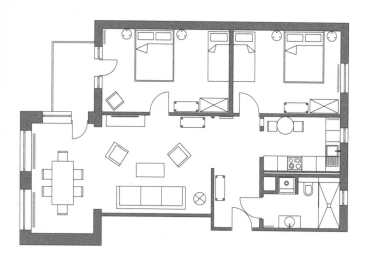

View of the bedroom with balcony. Detail of the kitchen. Interior view of the apartment.

INFORMATION. ARCHITECTS>
JENSEN & SKODVIN // 2009–2013.
HOTEL> 830 SQM // 20 GUESTS //
9 BEDROOMS // 9 BATHROOMS.
ADDRESS> ALSTAD, VALLDAL,
NORWAY.
WWW.JUVET.COM

View of one cabin with floor-to-ceiling windows to enjoy views. One of the cabins in the surrounding nature. Main view of one cabin from below. Relaxation area with views.

Juvet Landscape Hotel

VALLDAL, NORWAY

Juvet, Europe's first landscape hotel, lies on a sheer riverbank, amongst birch, aspen, pine and nature-sculpted boulders. At first glance, the seven detached guest rooms seem modest and unassuming. But when guests open the door and go in, it's as if nature rushes in to greet them through the massive panoramic windows. They can almost feel the trees brushing against them, and the snow-white drops of spray from the Valldøla river on their faces.

Burtigarden at Alstad is one of the biggest, oldest farms in the area of inner Sunnmøre. The restored farm buildings form a historic frame around the modern cubes. Preserving the traditional farm milieu and cultivated landscape was a vital concern, while making way for the new with due care and consideration. The cowshed is now a dining room seating 50 people, while the farmhouse can accommodate 12 people. The reception and the events area are located in the barn.

View of one cabin in full harmony with the landscape. Interior view of the spa with fireplace. Detail of the glass wall with striking view of the valley. Interior view.

GETTING AROUND. JUVET LANDSCAPE HOTEL CAN BE EXPERIENCED IN MANY DIFFERENT WAYS. GUESTS CAN DO WHATEVER THEY FEEL LIKE – RELAX IN THE ROOM, LIE AROUND IN THE POOL AREA, EXPLORE THE EXCITING SURROUND-INGS. THEY CAN TAKE AN ORGANIZED TRIP, OR BLAZE THEIR OWN TRAILS: MOUNTAIN HIKING, WINTER SPORTS, WILDNESS CAMP, RAFTING ARE ALL POSSIBLE IN THIS WORLD HERITAGE SITE.

PORT X

PRAGUE, CZECH REPUBLIC

Main view. Interior view of the dining area.
Side view of the floating house.

Conceptual living on water, modern houseboat, unique piece of architecture, design object... PORT X is all that and more. Created by Czech studio Atelier SAD, its C-shaped curves not only define its visual character but also support the whole construction. Thoughtful selection of materials using laminate with a thin top layer of gel coat as the basic structural material ensures smooth functioning in the water. Consisting of six modules, it is easily dismountable and thus always ready for transport to a completely different location at any time.

Its panoramic full-length windows, spacious living room, outside terraces, and fully equipped kitchenette offer a blend of sophistication and independence. The houseboat features carefully selected top-brand design furnishing and state of the art technology including Bang & Olufsen hi-fi and other top quality audio-video equipment, including a smart control system. Sleeping on a king size Saffron bed made of strictly natural materials adds a whole new perspective to the experience. Two additional guests can make use of a quality Italian sofa bed from VIbieffe, which also offers great sleeping comfort.

INFORMATION. ARCHITECTS>
ATELIER SAD // 2013. FLOATING
HOUSE> 150 SQM // FROM 2 TO
4 GUESTS // 1 BEDROOM //
1 BATHROOM. ADDRESS> V PRISTAVU,
PRAGUE, CZECH REPUBLIC.
WWW.PORTX.CZ

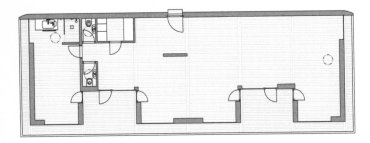

GETTING AROUND. THE SURROUNDING AREA OF HOLEŠOVICE OFFERS A VAST SELECTION OF INTERESTING ARCHITECTURE, CULTURAL HOTSPOTS LIKE THE DOX CENTER FOR CONTEMPORARY ART, LA FABRIKA, JATKA 78 AT THE VIBRANT HISTORIC HOLEŠOVICE MARKET PLACE, AND LAST BUT NOT LEAST, THE NATIONAL GALLERY IN VELETRŽNÍ PALÁC. GASTRONOMY ALSO RULES IN THIS NEIGHBORHOOD – NEW TRENDY PLACES KEEP APPEARING EVERY YEAR – TRY HOME KITCHEN, PHIL'S CORNER OR MARRE.

Night view from the water. Floor plan.
View of the bathroom.

View of the bedroom. Detail of the living room
opening to the terrace. The living room.

View of the living room. Night view of the back façade from the garden. The building from the street.

INFORMATION. ARCHITECTS> DEPA ARCHITECTS + MARGARIDA LEITÃO // 2016. APARTMENT BUILDING> 382 SQM // 12 GUESTS // 4 APARTMENTS // 4 BATHROOMS. ADDRESS> PORTO, PORTUGAL. WWW.AIRBNB.DE/ROOMS/11132494

Casa do Rosário

PORTO, PORTUGAL

Casa do Rosário had almost everything: a comfortable scale, an appealing composition, and a captivating atmosphere. The big challenge was to keep its domestic spirit, and to refrain from a major design or a deep intervention. Taking this into consideration, the project approach was essentially a work of preservation, keeping the original references intact and repurposing what had been negatively changed over the years. The main façade was restored and the original yellow tiles that were missing were put back in place while the back façade was completely renewed as it consisted of additional volumes with no constructive quality. Following the strategy that was adopted for the whole building, the back façade is therefore a composition that assembles a wooden structure with reclaimed fanlights that were adapted for use as doors and windows. The colors of the existing façade served as an inspiration for the tenuous color scheme of the interiors such as the winter gardens with the yellow geometric-patterned hydraulic tiles on the floor. Most furniture was assembled locally and designed specifically for the house mixing new and reused wooden elements from furniture and other architectural elements that were found in the house and had no function at the moment. Similar to many typical Porto buildings from the 19th century, there is a private patio on the back with a garden and a small backyard studio that also share the same design principles of the house.

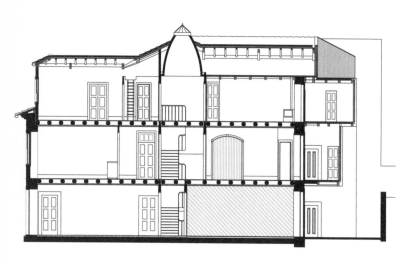

GETTING AROUND. THE ARTS DISTRICT, WHERE CASA DO ROSÁRIO IS LOCATED, HAS BECOME A MEETING POINT FOR ALL THOSE WHO ENJOY ART AND INNOVATION. NEW EXHIBITS ARE REGULARLY INAUGURATED SIMULTANEOUSLY, WHILE STREET ENTERTAINMENT ATTRACTS A WIDE AUDIENCE OF ART LOVERS, INVESTORS, ARTISTS, FOLLOWERS OF ALTERNATIVE WAYS OF LIFE, AND MANY ONLOOKERS. THERE ARE ALSO MANY RESTAURANTS, BOOK SHOPS, AND RETRO-COOL FURNITURE SHOPS, WITH ALTERNATIVE DECORATION, DESIGN, FASHION, MUSIC, AND MORE.

Interior view of the dining room. Cross section.
View of the new terrace on top of the building.
One of the bedrooms.

INFORMATION. ARCHITECTS>
PLATFORM 5 // 2016. HOUSE>
165 SQM + 20 SQM BOATHOUSE //
8 GUESTS // 4 BEDROOMS //
2 BATHROOMS. ADDRESS>
WROXHAM, NORFOLK, ENGLAND.
WWW.BACKWATERNORFOLK.CO.UK

Backwater

NORFOLK, ENGLAND

Backwater is a stunning and sustainable detached family home replacing an outdated bungalow in a secluded lagoon in the Norfolk Broads. Platform 5 Architects' design references vernacular forms and materials while establishing a contemporary counterpoint to more traditional neighboring houses. The house is raised above flood levels and arranged as three low-rise bays, whose pitched roofs echo nearby working boatsheds. Each bay has a different volume and is carefully aligned to provide different views across the wetland landscape. Untreated timber shingles give a warm and textured look to the entrance façade that will weather over time, while blackened shingles clad the roofscape and side walls to express the form as an abstract folded plane. Deep eaves on the waterside emphasize the bold contemporary silhouette and provide sheltered external areas that are useable across the seasons. Inside, a simple broken layout allows for flexible living through the use of timber sliding doors. The central bay contains a kitchen and dining area, and flows into the adjacent double-height living space. The bedrooms occupy the third bay and are split over two floors.

Exterior view of the house. Interior view. Details of the dining room. Main view of the house from the water.

The house nestled in the nature. One of the bedrooms. Cross section. View of the living room with large window.

GETTING AROUND. BACKWATER IS A CONTEMPORARY WATERSIDE HOLIDAY HOME IN A SERENE SETTING WITH PANORAMIC VIEWS OVER A PRIVATE LAGOON TEEMING WITH WILDLIFE. IT IS LOCATED IN THE HEART OF THE NORFOLK BROADS, A NATIONAL PARK OFFERING WILDLIFE AND LEISURE ACTIVITIES SUCH AS BOATING, WALKING, CYCLING AND FISHING. SEVERAL BEACHES IN THE VICINITY ARE GOOD FOR SWIMMING IN THE SUMMER AND SEAL WATCHING IN THE WINTER. GUESTS CAN MOOR THEIR BOATS ALONG THE EAST DECK FOR EASY ACCESS TO WROXHAM BROAD AND THE RIVER BURE.

INFORMATION. ARCHITECTS> MARC NAGEL AND CHRISTINA HOYER // 2018. HARBOR CRANE> 18 + 13 SQM // 2 GUESTS // 1 BEDROOM // 1 BATHROOM. ADDRESS> MOORING SANDTORHAFEN, AM SANDTORKAI, ENTRANCE BETWEEN 60 AND 62, HAFENCITY, HAMBURG, GERMANY. WWW.FLOATEL.DE

Main view of the HafenCity Hafenkran from the water. Detail of the collection of the Harry's bazaar. Great view of the Elbphilharmonie from the lounge area.

HafenCity Hafenkran

HAMBURG, GERMANY

Located in the heart of HafenCity, directly across from the Elbphilharmonie concert hall, the dockside crane was converted into a maritime hideaway. After nearly 70 years of carrying heavy loads, the crane is now a romantic getaway for couples. They can experience the harbor close up, but when the crane door closes, they are in a world of their own, far away from everyday life. It is not a five-star hotel, there is no lobby and no bell boy, yet nothing is missing. The style is simple, maritime and occasionally rather special, the furniture is functional, clever and almost every piece is one-of-a-kind.

The crane is not only the most exceptional accommodation in Hamburg, but is also home to the city's decidedly most peculiar museum, Harrys Hamburger Hafenbasar. The pontoon contains the erratic collection of the white-bearded captain Harry Rosenberg, may he rest in peace, who spent his entire life collecting the most unbelievable items from all around the world, either picking them up himself or receiving them as gifts from his seafaring friends. Today, the guests of the hideaway can visit the exhibition during its opening hours before retiring to their "cabin". Spending the night at this magical place is definitely a very special experience.

GETTING AROUND. REGARDLESS OF WHETHER YOU ARE VISITING HAMBURG AS A TOURIST AND WANT TO SEE AS MUCH OF IT AS POSSIBLE, OR IF YOU HAVE BEEN LIVING FOR 50 YEARS IN THE CITY AND WANT TO ESCAPE YOUR EVERYDAY ROUTINE, THE HARBOR CRANE IS LOCATED VERY CENTRALLY WITHIN WALKING DISTANCE TO THE MAIN STATION, THE MÖNCKEBERGSTRASSE SHOPPING DISTRICT, AND THE ELBPHILHARMONIE. AT THE SAME TIME, IT ALLOWS GUESTS TO FORGET THE WORLD AROUND THEM. ANYONE ENTERING THE FLOATING HARBOR CRANE IMMEDIATELY FEELS ITS SPECIAL MAGIC.

Exterior view of the crane. Side view. Detail of the maritime furniture and fireplace.

Interior view of the sleeping area with striking lighting. Detail of the terrace. General view.

INFORMATION. ARCHITECT>
FREDERICO VALSASSINA // 2013.
HOUSE> 332.25 SQM //
4–6 GUESTS // 4 BEDROOMS //
5 BATHROOMS. ADDRESS>
COLARES, SINTRA, PORTUGAL.
WWW.BOUTIQUE-HOMES.COM/
VACATION-RENTALS/EUROPE/
PORTUGAL/CASA-DA-RAMPA-
SINTRA-PORTUGAL

*View of the house surrounded by the forest. Interior
view of the kitchen. Detail of the courtyard.*

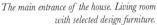
The main entrance of the house. Living room with selected design furniture.

Casa da Rampa

SINTRA, PORTUGAL

Situated within the Sintra-Cascais National Park along the far west Atlantic coast of Portugal, the house sets a distinct contemporary tone among the pines. The eye-catching horizontal silhouette is in serene balance with its rural environment. Completed in 2013, the white-on-white structure is composed of interconnecting spaces that focus outwards with brightly illuminated interiors that respond to the landscape. Walls of windows, strong linear lines and a minimalist, unadorned approach create a sense of space and serenity. Divided into individual "boxes", the living and dining areas overlook the forest and the sleek fully equipped kitchen features a wall-sized pivoting glass door that creates an interaction between indoor and outdoor spaces.

Each of the four en suite bedrooms faces the wilderness and there is an additional room design specifically for children. Expertly selected design touches include original Eames Vitra lounge chairs, Jielde lamps, a Stuv fireplace, and a collection of 1960s vintage treasures.

View of the large glass wall from the courtyard. Detail of one of the bathrooms. Main view of the house from the forest.

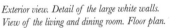

Exterior view. Detail of the large white walls.
View of the living and dining room. Floor plan.

GETTING AROUND. THE AREA IS
LINED WITH EXCELLENT BEACHES
WHILE THE NEARBY ROCA CAPE IS A
DRAMATIC HEADLAND FORMATION
ON THE WESTERNMOST POINT OF
THE EUROPEAN MAINLAND. LISTED
AS A UNESCO WORLD HERITAGE
SITE AND LOCATED HALF AN HOUR
FROM LISBON, THE CULTURAL
HERITAGE OF THE TOWN OF SINTRA
INCLUDES BOTH MOORISH AND
EUROPEAN INFLUENCES. LINED
WITH GREAT SHOPS, CAFES AND
HISTORIC SPLENDOR, SINTRA IS
BEST EXPLORED BY FOOT.

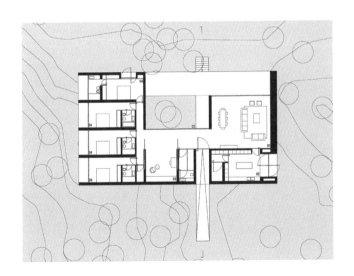

INFORMATION. ARCHITECT>
JONATHAN TUCKEY DESIGN // 2014.
HOUSE> 100 SQM // 6 GUESTS //
3 BEDROOMS // 2 BATHROOMS.
ADDRESS> ANDERMATT,
SWITZERLAND.
WWW.ANDERMATTCHALET.COM

Main view of the house surrounded by snow.
Detail of the dining area. View of kitchen
with double height.

Halbhaus

ANDERMATT, SWITZERLAND

The house lost its "other half" 40 years ago to a car park, and has since been known in the village as the "Halbhaus" (half house). In 2012, it was bought to be used as a base for skiing, climbing and hiking in the region – an escape into the Alps. The newly remodeled Halbhaus designed by Jonathan Tuckey Design represents the core concepts of this London-based studio. It is about materiality, juxtaposing new and old, and making historic structures feel alive and valued today. As a fragment, the building has a particular poetic quality now highlighted by its sloped ceilings that create a feeling of an attic hideaway. In the existing 17th-century chalet building the living rooms were on the raised ground floor and the bedrooms on

the first floor. The attic and basement were both used for storage. Like many houses of this generation, ceiling heights were very low (1.8 meters), the rooms were dark, and the building was not insulated. Despite these limitations, the appeal of the house was the simplicity of its construction: a stone base with a timber frame above. This traditional framework was ideal for the timeless pleasures of cooking, eating, laughing and sleeping. Like neighboring properties, the house was conceived as a series of open "communal" spaces. This meant that the spaces invited a more open-ended use as opposed to a set function. The house is furnished with a mix of new and old furniture and paintings from England, Scandinavia, and Poland.

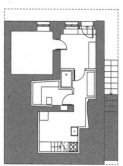

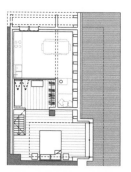

GETTING AROUND. ANDERMATT IS LOCATED AT 1,500 METERS AND SURROUNDED BY 3,000-METER MOUNTAINS. IN WINTER, IT OFFERS SOME OF THE BEST SKIING IN THE ALPS AND IS PARTICULARLY WELL-KNOWN FOR ITS OFF-PISTE AND SKI-TOURING. THE CABLE CAR IS A FIVE MINUTE WALK FROM THE HOUSE AND WHEN THE SNOW IS RIGHT IT IS POSSIBLE TO SKI TO THE FRONT DOOR. IN THE SUMMER, ANDERMATT IS A BASE FOR MOUNTAIN AND ROAD BIKING (FURKA, OBERALP, SUSTEN, GOTTHARD, GRIMSEL PASSES), MOUNTAINEERING, CLIMBING, HIKING, PARAGLIDING AND GOLF.

Relax area with fireplace. Floor plans.
Night view of the house. One of the bedrooms.

INFORMATION. ARCHITECTS> ATELIER MUTO - ARQUITETURA E ENGENHARIA // 2017. 5 CABINS> 22 SQM EACH // 2 GUESTS PER CABIN // 1 BEDROOM EACH // 1 BATHROOM EACH. ADDRESS> OUTÃO, SETÚBAL, PORTUGAL. WWW.VISITSETUBAL.COM.PT/EN/ HOTEIS/ECOPARQUE-DO-OUTAO

Treehouse Spot

SETÚBAL, PORTUGAL

JULAR has installed five Treehouse Spot units at the Outão Campsite, in Setúbal, Portugal.

This comprehensive project aims to provide the region with quality accommodation, in harmony with the surrounding landscape. The Treehouse Spot modular house is in essence a model of communion with nature. Wood prevails as the main building material, and all its components are PEFC-certified. Quality, comfort and thermal efficiency are ensured by a careful selection of materials and applied finishing. The easy assembly of Treehouse Spot is also one of the characteristics of this model, allowing it to be placed at any location fully assembled and ready to use.

Exterior view of the cabins. Large window with sea view. The cabins nestled in the surrounding landscape. Night view.

Night view of the main façade. The patio surrounded by wooden slats. Interior view of the kitchen. Floor plan.

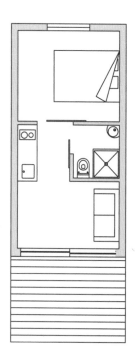

GETTING AROUND. LOCATED IN SETÚBAL, THE OUTÃO CAMPSITE IS PART OF THE MAGNIFICENT SERRA DA ARRÁBIDA NATURAL PARK IN WHICH MANY MEDITERRANEAN TREE SPECIES SUCH AS HOLM OAK, CORK OAK AND OAK FLOURISH. THE FAUNA IS QUITE DIVERSE BUT MOST COMMON ARE WILD CATS, FOXES, HARES, AND BONELLI'S EAGLES. THE VIEW IS BREATHTAKING – IT INCLUDES THE ESTUARY OF THE SADO RIVER, THE PENINSULA OF TROIA, AND THE MAGNIFICENT BEACHES OF PORTINHO DA ARRÁBIDA, GALAPOS AND FIGUEIRINHA.

Side view of the cabins. Detail of the terrace opening to the sea.

INFORMATION. ARCHITECTS>
STUDIOARTE // 2017. HOUSE>
168.86 SQM // 8 GUESTS //
4 BEDROOMS // 5 BATHROOMS.
ADDRESS> VALE DE AREIA,
FERRAGUDO, LAGOA, ALGARVE,
PORTUGAL.
WWW.CASAXYZA.COM

Casa XYZA

ALGARVE, PORTUGAL

This renovation project of a coastal house built in the 1980s aims to respect the footprint and pure essence of the existing building, consisting of various levels with different functions.

The approach is based on cleaning up the spaces with a pure, minimal, modern, Mediterranean, coastal inspiration and touch. The new functional program incorporates four ensuite bedrooms, open living area/kitchen, lounge-style outdoor kitchen, and a top platform with decking, a renewed pool and a connection to a top terrace on top of the house.

View of the kitchen and terrace. The living room with minimal Mediterranean style. View of the dining room. Main view of the house.

View of the bright double bedroom.
Detail of the lamp. Floor plan.

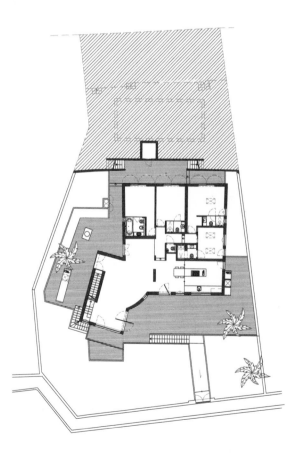

GETTING AROUND. CASA XYZA IS LOCATED ON AN ELEVATION POINT IN THE FISHING VILLAGE OF FERRAGUDO. FROM THE HOUSE'S LOCATION IT IS POSSIBLE TO SEE THE SEA AND REACH SEVERAL NEARBY BEACHES WITHIN ONLY 5 MINUTES OF WALKING. THE HOUSE FACES THE COASTAL PART OF THE CITY OF PORTIMÃO. THE MAIN INTERESTING BEACHES AROUND IT INCLUDE PRAIA GRANDE, PINTADINHO, AND CANEIROS, AMONG OTHERS. A NICE TRIP IS A BOAT VISIT TO THE CAVES.

View of living and dining area. View of terrace and swimming pool from above.

INFORMATION. ARCHITECTS>
ÁBATON // 2010. HOUSE> 322 SQM //
FROM 2 TO 16 GUESTS // 4 DOUBLE
BEDROOMS AND 1 DORMITORY //
4 BATHROOMS.
ADDRESS> CÁCERES, SPAIN.
WWW.ABATON.ES/EN/RENTAL

*View of the garden and pool. Detail of the long
kitchen counter. Living room with fireplace.
Main view of the house with local stone and
large wooden shutters.*

Estate in Extremadura

CÁCERES, SPAIN

Located in a privileged environment in the province of Cáceres, the goal was to transform an abandoned stable into a family home in a way that would be consistent with and respectful of the environment. At the end, the building was rebuilt from scratch due to the state of the stable. High on a hill and far from the public water and electricity grid, photovoltaic and hydro power systems were added (weighted toward solar in summer and hydro in winter), while keeping energy consumption low.

The building is located underneath two streams that flow year round providing it with pure water for drinking and bathing. The swimming pool acts as a holding tank for use in irrigation. Inside, nature has been incorporated into almost every room in the house: bathrooms feature views of the interior patio and its stone water fountain, while bedrooms have huge picture windows overlooking the countryside. The architecture was kept in the same location and the same materials were also used, although, given the building's crumbling state, the façade was rebuilt with a mix of cement and local stone. Inside, supporting walls were replaced by light metal pillars, the haylofts in the upper area were converted into bedrooms, and an enormous multipurpose central lounge was created. The result is a mix of modern cement and iron beams that coexist excellently with well-worn stone, weather-beaten wood, and local rock.

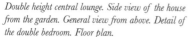
Double height central lounge. Side view of the house from the garden. General view from above. Detail of the double bedroom. Floor plan.

GETTING AROUND. MANY FANTASTIC AND FUN TREKKING TRAILS NEAR THE HOUSE RANGE FROM ONE HOUR TO TEN HOURS OF WALKING IN THE MOUNTAIN WITHOUT SEEING TRACES OF HUMANS. FOREST, HIGH MOUNTAINS, LONG DISTANCE VIEWS, BIG ROCKS, STREAMS, WILD GOAT (CABRA HISPÁNICA), WILD BOARS, EAGLES, VULTURES, FOX, SHEEP, COWS… OTHER THINGS TO DO AROUND "EL TORIL" ARE RELATED TO THE SURROUNDING UNTOUCHED NATURE AND SECLUDED PLACES OR HISTORICAL PLACES LIKE THE MONASTERIO DE YUSTE OR THE OLD TOWN OF CÁCERES, A UNESCO WORLD HERITAGE SITE.

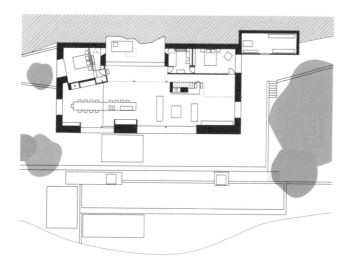

INFORMATION. ARCHITECTS>
VOAR ARQUITECTURA // 2012.
HOUSE> 800 SQM // 14 GUESTS //
7 BEDROOMS // 7 BATHROOMS.
ADDRESS> ARRAIOLOS, PORTUGAL.
WWW.VILLAEXTRAMUROS.COM

Exterior view from the swimming pool.
Detail of the pop interior decoration. View
of the private terrace.

Villa Extramuros

ARRAIOLOS, PORTUGAL

Built on a slope on the outskirts of an ancient town and surrounded by an extensive olive grove, Villa Extramuros manifests a picturesque contrast between wild nature and modernist shapes. Echoing the esthetic concepts of Mediterranean houses, yet deriving inspiration from the clear lines of contemporary architecture, the dwelling blends tradition and modernity to generate something entirely new.

Spreading over two floors, the façade gives the building a distinctive and abstract look. Inside the white cube, a large patio introduces generous light and creates a harmonious relationship with the exterior. Some parts of the ceiling, walls, and even the entrance doors are lined with cork, lending a warm, welcoming and sensual atmosphere, enhanced by the pop interior decoration consisting of furniture and art of the 1950s until today. Villa Extramuros offers five rooms with private terraces, large views on Arraiolos and cork tree covered hills, and since 2018, two contemporary cork "cabanons" are nested between olive trees and granite blocks, at a short distance from the stunning infinity pool and the main villa.

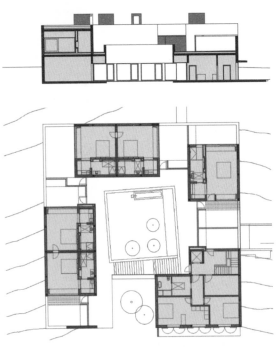

GETTING AROUND. VILLA EXTRAMUROS IS LOCATED ONLY 15 MINUTES FROM EVORA, A WORLD HERITAGE SITE, BUT ALL OF ALENTEJO IS RICH IN HISTORIC CITIES, TRADITIONAL VILLAGES, MEGALITHIC AND ROMAN REMAINS, SCENIC LANDSCAPES, AND NATURAL PARKS. PRIVATE GUIDED TOURS AND EXCURSIONS CAN BE ARRANGED. VILLA EXTRAMUROS IS AT A SHORT DISTANCE OF EXCELLENT FAMILY-OWNED WINERIES AND HAS ALSO CONNECTIONS TO HIGH-END HORSE FARMS. APART FROM THE VILLA'S INFINITY POOL, THE ATLANTIC OCEAN IS ONLY 45 MINUTES AWAY.

Main view from the garden. Cross section and floor plan. Panoramic view from the terrace.

View of the bedroom with large window. Relaxation area in the patio. Night view.

INFORMATION. ARCHITECT>
CLAUDIO BELTRAME // 2017.
TREE HOUSE> 70 SQM // 4 GUESTS //
2 BEDROOMS // 2 BATHROOMS.
ADDRESS> MALBORGHETTO, ITALY.
WWW.FACEBOOK.COM/MALGAPRIU

Pigna

MALBORGHETTO, ITALY

In one of the oldest and largest forests of Italy, where spruce tree wood is used to make violins and other musical instruments for its quality, this mountain retreat has been opened recently. The project aimed to create a structure that would not only be a refuge for people, but also a natural element in its environment, a mimesis of its surrounding. From the tree to the tree. The concept is based on an architectural competition in 2014, and only a couple of years later it was implemented in the Italian Alps near Tarvisio (at the border with Austria and Slovenia).

There are two tree houses that are developed on three levels, rising ten meters above the ground. The first level at four meters above ground is a panoramic covered terrace. The second level is on top of the stairs that lead indoors through two large sliding glass doors. There is a living room in front of a small kitchen and a bathroom. A stairway leads to the bedroom on the third floor. A double bed lies under a round skylight on top of the pinecone for guests to watch the stars above. The structure is completely made of CLT wood insulated with wooden fiber and covered in small larch timber shingles that can easily follow the curvature of the tree houses. All wood is sourced from the Alpe Adria area, which is expected to become the world's first organically farmed bioregion.

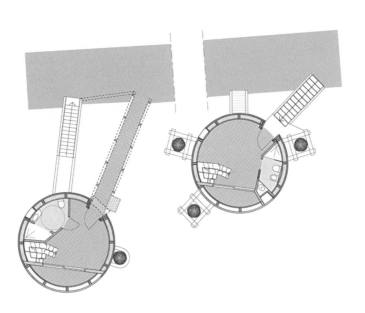

GETTING AROUND. THE AREA AROUND THE TREE HOUSE IS LOCATED 1,200 METERS ABOVE SEA LEVEL IN THE DOLOMITES, A UNESCO WORLD HERITAGE SITE. HIKERS REACH THE AREA AFTER A WALK OF A COUPLE OF HOURS; TOURISTS COME DAILY, ESPECIALLY DURING THE FULL MOON WHEN LOCAL GUIDES TAKE SMALL GROUPS TO A UNIQUE DINNER IN THE MIDDLE OF THE FOREST.

Winter view of the tree house. Floor plans.
Night view of the panoramic window.

View of the bedroom with curved wood
ceiling. The Pigna nestled in the surrounding
nature. Living area with balcony.

INFORMATION. ARCHITECTS>
LAURA AND NIELS ABEN // 2015.
MEDIEVAL BARN> 750 SQM //
24 GUESTS // 8 BEDROOMS //
5 BATHROOMS.
ADDRESS> LIEUDIT BASSIVIÈRE,
SAINT-ÉTIENNE-DE-VILLERÉAL,
FRANCE.
WWW.BASSIVIERE.COM

*Exterior view of the barn. Detail of the sleeping
alcoves. View of the living room with concrete floors.*

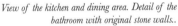
View of the kitchen and dining area. Detail of the bathroom with original stone walls..

Bassivière Barn Chic

SAINT-ÉTIENNE-DE-VILLERÉAL, FRANCE

Just south of the Dordogne in the region of Lot-et-Garonne in south-west France, Bassivière consists of five boutique holiday apartments in an original 17th-century farm-house. The old structures now house luxurious loft apartments with a contemporary industrial design. Offering a very relaxed and friendly atmosphere with plenty of space, the premises are embedded in nature yet offer all comforts of modern life. Original stone walls and oak ceiling beams are combined with urban steel, concrete floors and huge windows. It is comfortable yet at the same time has a very attractive modern-vintage feeling. Most guests come here for the good food, the good wine and a nice romantic getaway, especially in months like May, June, September,

and October when guests are mostly couples. In July and August many families come for their vacation.

The heated swimming pool is very popular, especially among the children. The outdoor play area with swings, a trampoline, table tennis and a zip line is a great meeting point for all.

The apartments cater to the needs of families and each of them offers a special sleeping area for the little ones. Guests can book massages at the massage room, take yoga lessons, and the owners can also organize wine tastings at one of the chateaus nearby. Furthermore, they offer art workshops for the entire family and also have art exhibitions on the premises.

General view of the living room with mezzanine.
View from the garden. Detail of the bathroom with
original sliding doors. View of the kitchen.

GETTING AROUND. PART OF THE
AQUITAINE REGION IN SOUTH-
WESTERN FRANCE, LOT-ET-GARONNE
IS RURAL FRANCE AT ITS BEST –
MEDIEVAL VILLAGES AND SUNFLOWER
FIELDS, PLUM ORCHARDS, QUIET
ROADS, AND SMALL FARMS IN GENTLY
ROLLING COUNTRYSIDE. THE NEAREST
VILLAGE IS MEDIEVAL VILLERÉAL WITH
ITS COLORFUL FARMERS' MARKET. IT IS
ALSO CLOSE TO OTHER PICTURESQUE
TOWNS LIKE MONFLANQUIN AND
MONPAZIER, AND THE IMPRESSIVE
CHATEAU DE BIRON. THE FAMOUS
DORDOGNE AREA, WITH ITS CAVES,
CASTLES AND PREHISTORIC SITES, IS
RIGHT NEXT DOOR.

INFORMATION. ARCHITECTS>
TARA ARCHITEKTEN // 2016–2017.
HOTEL> 4735.51 SQM // 86 GUESTS //
43 BEDROOMS // 43 BATHROOMS.
ADDRESS> ST. KATHREINSTRASSE,
HAFLING, BOLZANO, ITALY.
WWW.HOTEL-MIRAMONTI.COM

Miramonti Boutique Hotel

BOLZANO, ITALY

Only 20 minutes by car from the bustling city of Merano, the Miramonti Boutique Hotel resembles at first glance a rock jutting from the mountain. It is so cleverly integrated into nature with carefully chosen matching materials that this part of the hotel is almost entirely integrated into the dark mountain rock on which it is built. The dark outer skin immediately conveys intimacy and makes the clearly structured incisions of the terraces appear like ducts that lead into the depth. Inside the building, the extensive view resulting from the prominent position on the rock immediately catches the attention. In the hall and the dining room only glass separates the guests from the horizon. On the extensive terrace also, nothing impedes the view and only an infinity pool at its outer edge stops guests that do not suffer from vertigo.

The generous terraces with floor-to-ceiling panorama windows offer views of the surrounding green forests and mountain peaks. In 2017, the star-gazing rooms were added, furnished in a satiated blue. Arranged under a multifaceted sloping roof, they expand the room experience in all dimensions.

Panoramic view from the spa area. Interior view of one bedroom. Details of the floor-to-ceiling windows. Main view of the building from below.

Interior view of one room. Exterior view of the terrace. Floor plan.

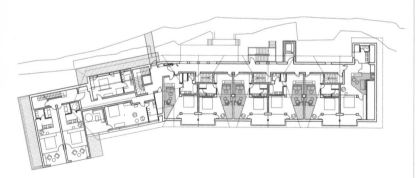

GETTING AROUND. MERANO, THE CITY OF CULTURE WITH MANY HIDDEN VENUES, VARIOUS MARKETS AND RESTAURANTS HAS MUCH TO OFFER: THE THERMAL SPA, THE GARDENS OF TRAUTTMANSDORFF CASTLE, THE "ÖTZI" MUSEUM, THE LABYRINTH GARDEN, WINE TASTINGS AND HORSE RACES, ARE ALL EXPERIENCES NOT TO BE MISSED. VARIOUS LAKES INVITE SWIMMERS WITH THREE IMPRESSIVE WATERFALLS IN THE VICINITY. THE HIKING AREA MERANO 2,000 OFFERS MANY TRAILS AND MOUNTAIN HUTS.

Striking view of the surrounding mountains from the infinity pool. One of the bedrooms.

INFORMATION. ARCHITECT>
IÑAKI LEITE // 2013. VILLA> 390 SQM //
8 GUESTS // 4 BEDROOMS //
4 BATHROOMS. ADDRESS> A POBRA
DO CARAMIÑAL, GALICIA, SPAIN.
WWW.DEZANOVEHOUSE.COM

Dezanove House

GALICIA, SPAIN

The interior of this architectural award-winning house has been carefully designed with bespoke furniture, great attention to details and the highest quality. The house has three double bedrooms, four bathrooms, main kitchen, living room and a study. The design and architectural inspiration came from the reclaimed eucalyptus wood of the "bateas". These are the wooden platforms for mussel production floating in the estuary, which constitute one of the most important local industries. The wood has been in use for 25 years and it took a very long time to collect as the local fishermen were gradually renewing the platforms. The shape and material of the house recalls the booths of the old bateas, and similarly to them, some parts of the house appear to float. Some of the premises to be achieved by the house were respect for its natural surroundings, environmental friendliness, maximum energy efficiency, great natural light and a relaxing atmosphere. As a special feature, the very spacious kitchen plays an important role as a key social space in the core of the house.

View of the living room with fireplace. The kitchen with a central island workstation. Panoramic window in the living room. Main view from the garden.

View of the bedroom. Detail of the wood façade.
Bathroom. Floor plan. View of the stairs.

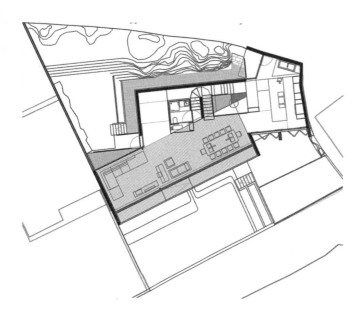

GETTING AROUND. THIS GEM IS
LOCATED IN A LITTLE KNOWN
REGION OF SPAIN – GALICIA – WITH
EXCELLENT RESTAURANTS, MARKETS
AND NATURE. ACROSS A SEMI-
PRIVATE LANE THERE IS A QUIET
BEACH WITH CLEAR WATER. THE
HOUSE IS ONLY MINUTES FROM A
SAILING AND A DIVING SCHOOL. THE
NATURAL GROTTOES OF THE PEDRAS
RIVER AND OUTDOOR ACTIVITIES ARE
AVAILABLE NEARBY INCLUDING
CANYONING, HORSEBACK RIDING,
HIKING AND BOAT CHARTER IN THE
NATURE RESERVES OF THE CÍES
ISLANDS. SPECIAL ARRANGEMENTS
WITH WELL-KNOWN LOCAL CHEFS
AND A YACHT MASTER MAKE EVERY
STAY MEMORABLE.

INFORMATION. ARCHITECTS> FEILDEN FOWLES // 2013. HOUSE> 130 SQM // 9 GUESTS // 4 BEDROOMS // 3 BATHROOMS. ADDRESS> BUDE, CORNWALL, ENGLAND. WWW.VENN-FARM.CO.UK

Exterior view of the house. Detail of the façade. View of the large kitchen and dining room.

Bude Barn

CORNWALL, ENGLAND

The renovation of this cob barn adds another layer of history to a building that has been expanded and stitched together over the last 200 years. The project celebrates the rich material patchwork of cob, stone, concrete, and brick, keeping much of the existing fabric while inserting a new load-bearing timber frame.

The delineation between old and new elements is clearly distinguished in the external faces of the building. New openings are framed with precast concrete, while the roof stands independent of the existing walls through a new clerestory, set back from the cob surface. On top, vertical fins express this depth of construction and the rhythm of the internal structure, while providing additional solar protection and privacy to the upper floor.

Distinct from the rendered farmhouse and red brick cottage, the barn completes the ensemble of buildings around the farmyard.

GETTING AROUND. THE COB HAS TWO PRIVATE TERRACES AND A LARGE GRASSY GARDEN, PERFECT FOR FOOTBALL, AL FRESCO BREAKFASTS, OR EVENING SUNDOWNERS. THE BI-FOLD DOORS TO THE EASTERN TERRACE INTRODUCE THE OUTSIDE TO THE INSIDE, ALLOWING CHILDREN TO ROAM FREELY WHILE IN SAFE SIGHT OF PARENTS. GUESTS ARE INVITED TO COLLECT FRESH EGGS EVERY MORNING FROM FRIENDLY FREE-RANGE HENS.

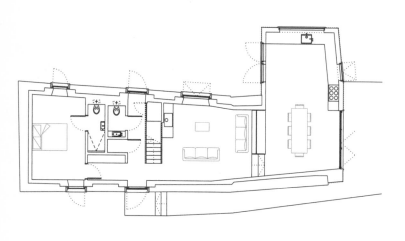

View of the kitchen. Floor plan.
View of the main entrance of the building.
Exterior view of the Bude Barn.

INFORMATION. ARCHITECTS>
VIPP // 2017. LOFT> 400 SQM //
4 GUESTS // 2 BEDROOMS //
1 BATHROOM. ADDRESS>
COPENHAGEN, DENMARK.
WWW.VIPP.COM/HOTEL

*View of the dining area. Living room with
fireplace. Detail of the Vipp kitchen island.
Interior view of the open space.*

Vipp Loft

COPENHAGEN, DENMARK

A 400 square meters curated design experience and perched atop the old printing factory from 1910 in Copenhagen's Islands Brygge area, Vipp Loft is an inviting urban habitat where design meets art. Conceptualized by Studio David Thulstrup, the high-sloped ceilings and grand volume of the light-filled Vipp Loft welcomes guests to a holistic home environment.

The moment they check in at the Vipp hotel, it is fully booked. That is because the Vipp hotel is not a hotel in the traditional sense. Instead of offering many rooms in one location, Vipp offers unique rooms at various destinations that all share the same goal: to invite people to experience firsthand Vipp's philosophy of good design in places out of the ordinary. The ambition is to offer a palette of destinations with rooms curated to guests who seek a one-off design experience, or customers who want to try out the Vipp kitchen in a home-away-from-home setting.

View of the double bedroom. The living room from above. General view of the loft. Bathroom with modern design furnitures.

GETTING AROUND. THE VIPP LOFT IS A TRUE DESIGN EXPERIENCE JUST 10 MINUTES FROM THE HEART OF COPENHAGEN. THE LOFT IS SITUATED AT THE HEART OF THE VIPP BRAND, ON THE TOP FLOOR OF THE VIPP OFFICE. GUESTS HAVE 400 SQM TO PLAY AROUND IN THE KITCHEN, LOUNGE ON THE COUCH, SOAK IN THE TUB, OR CATCH UP ON SOME READING IN THE LIBRARY. JUST NEXT DOOR ARE BAKERIES, COFFEE SHOPS AND THE COPENHAGEN HARBOR.

INFORMATION. ARCHITECTS>
ZEST ARCHITECTURE // 2013.
VILLA> 450 SQM // 10 GUESTS //
5 BEDROOMS // 4 BATHROOMS.
ADDRESS> GIRONA, SPAIN.
WWW.VILLA-CP.COM

*Interior view of the kitchen. Entrance door with the
villa's logo. Exterior view. Main view of the house
from the natural pool.*

Villa CP

GIRONA, SPAIN

This stylish Catalan farmhouse has been completely rebuilt as a sustainable modern eco-villa by the renowned Barcelona architects, ZEST Architecture. The exclusive restoration oozes quality and style. The outside area features fabulous Mediterranean gardens, an infinity bio-pool and miles of space all around. The cool, modern interiors with vivid textiles combine beautifully with classic mid-century furniture.

Summers here are hot and the ingenious geothermal installation cools the floors, providing a pleasant temperature throughout the house without the problems associated with air conditioning. The natural bio-pool uses fresh mountain water from an on-site well. The water is filtered and cleaned by aquatic plants such as water lilies, which are in a separate zone from the swimming area. Swimming in natural water with no salt or chemicals makes the skin and hair feel fabulous!

*Interior view of the dining area opening
to the terrace. View of the living room.*

One bedroom. Sunset view from the infinity pool. Bathroom with panoramic window. Floor plan.

GETTING AROUND. THE HOUSE IS LOCATED IN THE GAVARRES NATIONAL PARK, NEAR GIRONA AND THE COSTA BRAVA'S FAMOUS SANDY BEACHES, AND JUST AN HOUR FROM BARCELONA. WALK OR CYCLE ALONG SHADED PATHS AND YOU'RE UNLIKELY TO COME ACROSS ANYONE ELSE FOR HOURS.

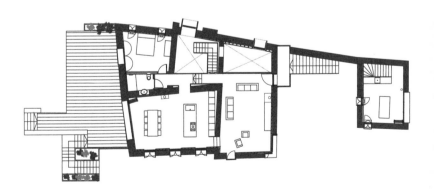

INFORMATION. ARCHITECTS>
FIEDERLING HABERSANG
ARCHITEKTEN // 2015.
HOUSE> 100 SQM // 6 GUESTS //
2 BEDROOMS // 2 BATHROOMS.
ADDRESS> SCHUTZ, GERMANY.
WWW.VULKANEIFELHAUS.COM

*View of the living room with fireplace. Detail of the
stairs in warm wood, as most of the furniture. View
of the living and dining room.*

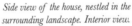
Side view of the house, nestled in the surrounding landscape. Interior view.

Haus in der Vulkaneifel

SCHUTZ, GERMANY

The timber house is located at the edge of a village in the Vulkaneifel (Volcanic Eifel) region. The interior layout of the house was derived from its location on a slope.
All rooms are separated from each other by slight elevations. From the entrance, the space spirals upwards around the central fireplace to the living room, the kitchen, a bedroom and finally to the gallery, from where the view is once again of the living room. Going downwards in the other direction, one first reaches the second bedroom, followed by the garden room with a second entrance towards the valley.

The seven different elevation levels and the sloped roof create attractive spatial units with alternating depths and widths, offering views throughout the house and of the surrounding landscape.

*Main view of the house. Living room with
panoramic view of the mountains.*

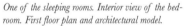
One of the sleeping rooms. Interior view of the bedroom. First floor plan and architectural model.

GETTING AROUND. THE VOLCANIC EIFEL IS AN UNSPOILED NATURAL LANDSCAPE IN WESTERN GERMANY. WITH ITS STRIKING VOLCANIC CONES, THE ASSOCIATED MAAR LAKES, AND DEEP VALLEYS, IT OFFERS NATURE ENTHUSIASTS, HIKERS AND BICYCLISTS MANY VANTAGE POINTS. THE HOUSE IS LOCATED ON AN OPEN SOUTHERN SLOPE WITH A FANTASTIC VIEW OF THE ALLUVIAL MEADOWS OF THE SMALL KYLL RIVER AND THE FORESTED SLOPES. IN THE SUMMER, GUESTS CAN SWIM IN THE MEERFELDER MAAR.

INFORMATION. ARCHITECTS> SOFIE LACHAERT & LUC DHANIS AND SEVERAL ARTISTS AND DESIGNERS // 2017. FORMER SHIPYARD> 3,535 SQM // 2 GUESTS // 1 BEDROOM // 1 BATHROOM. ADDRESS> ST.-JOZEFSTRAAT, TIELRODE, BELGIUM. WWW.ATELIERLACHAERTDHANIS.COM

Atelier Lachaert Dhanis

TIELRODE, BELGIUM

Experience art in a new way by sojourning in an artwork by the artist duo Sofie Lachaert and Luc Dhanis: a unique experience amidst boundary-breaking objects in a dialogue of the mundane and the sublime. "Sharpen your senses", the working and living habitat of the artists is embedded in a beautiful riverscape and situated on the site of a reinvigorated shipyard.

Tracks of the industrial past were laboriously processed into the contemporary setting it is today. This crossbreeding of the here and now with the past creates a transcendental atmosphere. Guests are invited to step into the experience and "sleep with their eyes wide open" in an oasis of tranquility.

They can stay in the "one and only" suite – a wonderful sleeping accommodation with a king-size bed made up with the finest Belgian linen, a bathroom with a rainfall shower, and Japanese bathtub.

Other spaces are also freely accessible: the workshop, a spacious meeting area with a four-meter-long inviting table, a breakfast area bathed in subtle northern light, a shelter overlooking the wide and semi-wild garden, and an impressive loft space with high windows with a view of a 17th-century chapel. A memorable experience à la carte can be arranged for a specific experience that transcends the mundane with services tailored to guests' needs.

GETTING AROUND. THE VENUE IS NESTLED IN A PHOTOGENIC RIVER LANDSCAPE IN FLANDERS, IDEAL FOR WALKING OR CYCLING AND ENJOYING THE TRANQUILITY OF NATURE. IT IS PERFECTLY SITUATED WITHIN THE GOLDEN TRIANGLE OF ANTWERP-BRUSSELS-GHENT.

Interior view of the dining room. View of the art collection. Detail of the wooden stairs.

The ephemeral room. View of the Japanese bathtub. Detail of the bathroom.

INFORMATION. ARCHITECTS>
A BIRO D.O.O. (VODUSEK & DOLECEK)
// 2016. HOUSE> 160 SQM // 6 GUESTS
// 3 BEDROOMS // 2 BATHROOMS.
ADDRESS> PRESERJE 10, BRANIK,
SLOVENIA.
WWW.VILA-MRAVLJEVI.SI

*View of the house from the garden. Detail of the
terrace with swimming pool. Exterior view.*

Vila Mravljevi

BRANIK, SLOVENIA

On a hill between the Vipava Valley on one side and the Karst plateau on the other lies the idyllic village of Mravljevi, the home of Villa Mravljevi. There were two objects: the old stone house, object A, and the outbuilding, object B. The existing residential housing was reconstructed, while the outbuilding was demolished and a new object, object B, was built as an auxiliary building. Each space reflects its own character.

In its essence, object A is a stony cottage with a smaller sloped gabled roof, typical of the traditional construction in the area. The basic structure of the house was left untouched, while the worn-out wooden plate had to be replaced by a concrete one. The object remains as it was, apart from some elements such as its steel staircase.

The concrete volume of object B floats over the existing stone wall with an intentionally exaggerated roof slope, giving the impression of not belonging to the area. However, combined with the existing stone structure, it blends imperceptibly with nature. The equipment of the facility is a combination of ancient and modern. A suspended, floating open fireplace in front of a glass façade, offering beautiful views of the Karst plateau in object B, and a modern rotating furnace, situated between the dining and living room in the object A, are also very impressive.

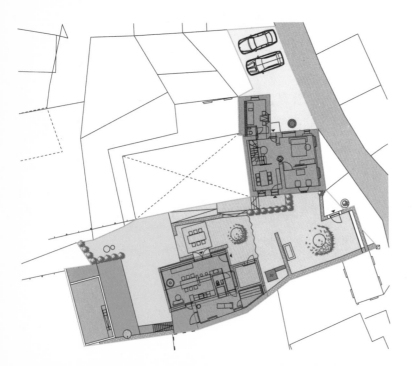

GETTING AROUND. MRAVLJEVI VILA IS SURROUNDED BY FERTILE LAND, THE HIGH KARST PLATEAU AND VIPAVA HILLS. THIS DIVERSE LANDSCAPE OFFERS MANY OPPORTUNITIES FOR OUTDOOR ACTIVITIES. THE REGION IS FAMOUS FOR ITS ORCHARDS, VINEYARDS AND HIGH-GRADE CUISINE. GUESTS CAN EMBARK ON A GOURMET TRIP TO NEARBY RESTAURANTS, OFFERING DELICACIES INFLUENCED BY KARST TRADITION, ITALIAN CUISINE AND OLD SLOVENIAN HERITAGE.

View of the living room with floating fireplace.
Floor plan. Interior view of the private sauna.

Interior view of the living room.
One of the bedrooms. Exterior view.

INFORMATION. ARCHITECTS> STUDIO LOT, VERONIKA OBERMEIER AND FORMAT ELF ARCHITEKTEN // 2014. 15 ROOMS AND HOUSES> 30,000 SQM // 26 GUESTS // 1 BEDROOM EACH // 1 BATHROOM EACH. ADDRESS> BAD BIRNBACH, NIEDERBAYERN, GERMANY. WWW.HOFGUT.INFO

Exterior view of the house. Detail of the bathroom. Night view of the house with outdoor fireplace.

Hofgut Hafnerleiten

BAD BIRNBACH, GERMANY

A few kilometers away from the town of Bad Birnbach in Bavaria, the Hafnerleiten estate is located in the middle of nature, offering 15 very individual accommodations. The seven themed houses and three vacation cottages as well as two pond suites and three individual rooms are each lovingly furnished in a unique style. Designed by the architect duo Hanninger and Maier of Format Elf, the three long houses that were opened in mid-2013 offer plenty of space and privacy, making them ideally suited for extensive stays. The houses located near the lake, forest and field, have a fully equipped kitchen, outdoor fireplace, and several terraces. Infrared cabins, snuggly bunks with a first-rate view of the starry sky and bathtubs with a natural panorama ensure maximum well-being in any kind of weather. Format Elf also designed the five wellness cubes that contain areas for massages, two saunas, and a relaxation room.

Originally established in 1999 as the region's first culinary school by Erwin Rückerl and his wife Anja Horn-Rückerl, culinary arts play an essential role in the estate. Cooking classes by the owner or four-course dinners in the evening ensure a familiar comfortable atmosphere that is pleasing to the heart of every gourmet. Deliberately going offline and doing nothing for a change is the motto at the Hafnerleiten estate.

GETTING AROUND. WALKS IN NATURE, THE CULINARY SCHOOL, OR THE IN-HOUSE LIBRARY, COUPLED WITH THE WELLNESS CUBES, OFFER RELAXATION AND A LITTLE TIME AWAY FROM BEING "ONLINE". IN THE ROOMS, SUITES, AND THEMATIC COTTAGES THE GUESTS ENJOY THEIR TIME WITHOUT THE DISTRACTION OF THE INTERNET, TELEVISION OR MOBILE PHONES, TO JUST RELAX AND REGAIN THEIR ENERGY. OF COURSE, NO ONE HAS TO DO COMPLETELY WITHOUT WI-FI, WHICH IS AVAILABLE FREE OF CHARGE IN THE MAIN HOUSE.

View of the house during sunset. Interior view of the living area. Detail of the terrace.

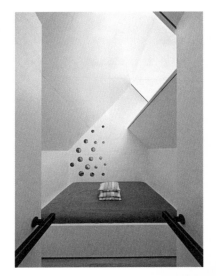

One of the sleeping rooms. View of the bedroom. Exterior view of the panoramic terrace.

INFORMATION. ARCHITECTS> THOMAS KRÖGER ARCHITEKTEN // 2014. HOUSE> 320 SQM + GUEST HOUSE 97 SQM // 15 GUESTS // 7 BEDROOMS // 4 BATHROOMS. ADDRESS> ORT FERGITZ 7, GERSWALDE, GERMANY. WWW.LANDHAUS-FERGITZ.COM

Main view from the garden. View of the living room. The large dining room with the wooden pyramid roof.

Landhaus Fergitz

GERSWALDE, GERMANY

In a small village in the heart of the Uckermark region, a large stable was converted into a country home with a separate vacation home. The stable was built 140 years ago of a mix of clinker brick masonry and timberwork, which was considered a very modern functional construction style at the time. It was later converted into a duplex.

One half of it was now redesigned by Thomas Kröger Architekten in a way that matched the architectural vocabulary of the house. It is a very stable building with thick stone walls, small windows, and a large wooden gate. The intrinsic beauty of the bearing structure and the spaciousness only appeared after the gutting of the building. At the center of the house is a double-height residential hall with a fireplace. Three new arched openings offer views of the surrounding green landscape. The large hall is not heated but surrounded by a closed heated space that allows only the smaller and more social areas to be used during the cold season.

Located on the gable end, the vacation home is accessed separately and additionally connected to the central hall. The intervention of the building skin is barely visible from the street. The upgrade created new openings to the private garden and the desired link between the interior and the exterior.

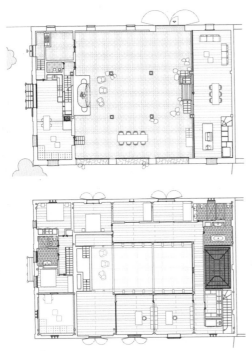

GETTING AROUND. THE COUNTRY COTTAGE IS LOCATED AT THE EDGE OF THE SMALL VILLAGE OF FERGITZ, AN HOUR NORTH OF BERLIN IN HILLY TERMINAL MORAINE LANDSCAPE. THE SMALL BEACH OF FERGITZ ON THE WEST SHORE OF THE OBERUCKERSEE IS 10 MINUTES AWAY. FERGITZ IS SITUATED IN THE EULENBERGE NATURE RESERVE, THE HABITAT OF MANY ENDANGERED PLANTS AND ANIMALS. IT IS ONE OF THE MOST BEAUTIFUL LANDSCAPES FOR OUTDOOR ACTIVITIES.

Night view of the main building. Ground and first floor plans. Detail of the wooden structure.

View of the kitchen. Detail of one of the bathrooms. Interior view of the house.

INFORMATION. ARCHITECT>
TIM BUSHE // 2012. HOUSE> 120 SQM //
6 GUESTS // 3 BEDROOMS //
2 BATHROOMS. ADDRESS> BECKLEY,
EAST SUSSEX, ENGLAND.
WWW.BOXWOOD-RETREAT.CO.UK

*Main view of the house from the garden. One of the
bedrooms. View of the kitchen and dining room.*

Boxwood

EAST SUSSEX, ENGLAND

Boxwood is a peaceful contemporary retreat set within quiet ancient woodland surrounded by mature oak, chestnut and pine trees offering a haven for a vast array of flora and fauna. The house has a spacious open-plan living/kitchen/dining space and utility room on the upper level that opens to two generous outdoor dining terraces. Three double bedrooms, accommodating up to six people, are located on the lower ground floor (sunk 1.2 meters into the ground) together with two large fully tiled family-size bathrooms, one en-suite to the main double bedroom.

With oak flooring used throughout the interior, the finishes are clean and light to maximize the use of natural light. Fiberglass marine-grade decking is used to create decks on the two end elevations. The house is highly thermally insulated and utilizes a low-energy air source heat pump to provide hot water and under-floor heating throughout. There is also a wood-burning stove for winter use.

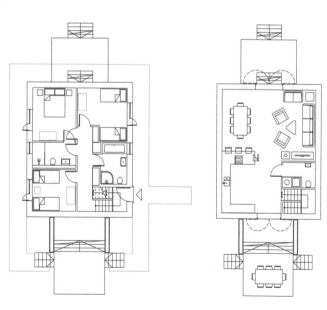

GETTING AROUND. THE HISTORIC HILLTOP TOWN OF RYE IS A TOP TOURIST ATTRACTION WITH ITS WINDING COBBLED STREETS, MEDIEVAL BUILDINGS AND RICH MIX OF SHOPS, GALLERIES, PUBS AND RESTAURANTS. HASTINGS TOWN, WITH THE NEW JERWOOD GALLERY, IS A 30-MINUTE DRIVE AWAY. FURTHER ALONG IS BEXHILL WITH THE DE LA WAR PAVILLION. DEREK JARMAN'S FISHERMAN'S HUT AND OTHER NOTABLE BUILDINGS SUCH AS NORD'S "SHINGLE HOUSE" ARE FOUND AT DUNGENESS. GREAT DIXTER, BODIAM CASTLE AND NATIONAL TRUST PROPERTIES AT SMALLHYTHE PLACE AND LAMB HOUSE IN RYE ARE ALL WITHIN EASY REACH.

Exterior view of the house. Floor plans.
View of the terrace. Living room with fireplace.

INFORMATION. ARCHITECTS>
FEATHERSTONE YOUNG // 2014.
MILL HOUSE> 412 SQM // 20 GUESTS //
7 BEDROOMS. ADDRESS> CLAYTON,
WEST SUSSEX, ENGLAND.
WWW.FEATHERSTONEYOUNG.COM

*Night view of the mill house. Detail of the stairs.
Interior view of the living room with fireplace.*

Jack Windmill

WEST SUSSEX, ENGLAND

Jack Windmill is a unique building complex which brings together a converted 19th-century milll house and granary on the site of two West Sussex landmarks, Jack and Jill Windmills. The site was renovated by London-based Featherstone Young in 2017.

Spanning five years, this complex and forensic renovation included the redevelopment of the 1960s mill house and the adjoining 19th-century granary into a 7-bedroom house. The design is radical whilst responsive to its sensitive location and follows the traditional black and white vernacular of Sussex mills, where white represents dynamic motion and black is static. Jack Windmill has had its five-story timber cap restored, and when

its sweeps are reinstated the pair's iconic silhouette on the ridge of the South Downs National Park will be preserved.

The ambition was to reuse and recycle all of the existing buildings. Interventions include the refurbishment of the 1960s dwelling, the addition of a new timber structure, and the insertion of new pop-up extensions on the roof of the house and granary, to open up important views between Jack and Jill.

The granary's interior has been designed along principles of what the practice calls "baggy space" – a larger, flexible central space around which more specific functions are grouped.

GETTING AROUND. THE BUILDING COMPLEX JACK WINDMILL IS GRADE II*. ALTHOUGH NOW IN PRIVATE OWNERSHIP, THE GRANARY CONTINUES TO HOST PUBLIC TOURS OCCASIONALLY AND THE SPACE HAS BEEN DESIGNED TO ACCOMMODATE LARGE PUBLIC GROUPS. THE ORIGINAL UNDERGROUND TUNNEL LINKING JACK WINDMILL TO THE GRANARY HAS BEEN RETAINED FOR FUTURE DEVELOPMENT.

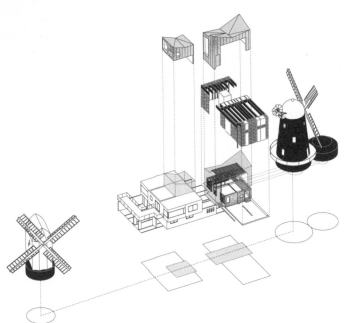

Main view of the house from the garden.
Axonometric view of the complex of buildings.
Detail of the renovated building.

View of the granary at sunset. View inside the granary. The living room with a large window.

INFORMATION. ARCHITECTS> HERBERT HUSSMANN ARCHITEKTEN // 2015. 2 HOUSES> 120 SQM EACH // 8 GUESTS HAUS PINE AND 6 GUESTS HAUS SAND // 4 BEDROOMS HAUS PINE AND 3 BEDROOMS HAUS SAND // 3 BATHROOMS. ADDRESS> ZWISCHEN DEN KIEFERN, DIERHAGEN, GERMANY. WWW.NEWHAUS.DE

NewHaus

DIERHAGEN, GERMANY

Located near the entrance to the Fischland-Darß-Zingst peninsula, the NewHaus vacation homes are situated on one of the few plots of land immediately connected to the beach of the Baltic Sea. The site is dominated by the vegetation of the bordering dune and the extensions of a nearby pine forest. Constructed of wood, the houses with the dark façades fit unobtrusively into this natural setting. The two structures have archetypal shapes and are slightly offset with their alignment reflecting that of the dune. This creates the greatest possible connection to the natural landscape from the main rooms.

Large terraces allow a flowing transition from indoors to outdoors. Designed based on a color concept of the Berlin-based artist Friederike Tebbe, the interior spaces are enlivened by a selection of artwork from the owners' collection. With a floor space of 120 square meters, the houses can each accommodate six to eight guests.

View of the living room with fireplace. The kitchen opening to the terrace. Detail of the colorful design furniture. General view of the houses from the garden.

View of the living room. Detail of one bedroom.
Floor plans. Exterior view.

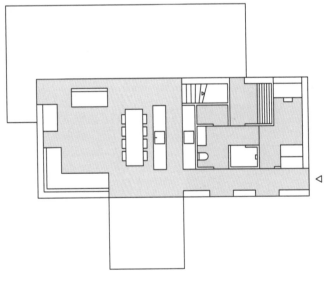

GETTING AROUND. THE BALTIC SEA BEACH RESORT OF DIERHAGEN IS SITUATED ON THE ENTRANCE TO THE FISCHLAND-DARSS-ZINGST PENINSULA, AROUND 35 KILOMETERS NORTHEAST OF ROSTOCK BETWEEN THE SEA AND THE INNER BAY. THE TWO HOUSES ARE SLIGHTLY AWAY FROM THE VILLAGE CENTER, IN AN IDYLLIC SETTING OF PINE FORESTS AND DUNES.

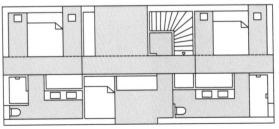

INFORMATION. ARCHITECTS>
MISHA SMITH & LUCY VOICE // 2016.
HOUSE> 4+2 GUESTS // 2 BEDROOMS
// 1 BATHROOM. ADDRESS>
KINGSBRIDGE, DEVON, ENGLAND.
WWW.MALTHOU.SE

The Malthouse

DEVON, ENGLAND

The Malthouse in Kingsbridge at the top of the Salcombe estuary in south Devon has been recently converted into unique accommodations. The shell of the original 19th-century building was carefully restored, while a new roof built from the reclaimed floor joists encloses a new modern interior. There is space for four in two double rooms, plus two children on the mezzanine. Originally built as part of the Phoenix brewery 200 years ago, the Malthouse is the oldest building in a terrace of cottages that have grown up around it. Dilapidated, neglected and unoccupied for many years, the building has been transformed into a light-filled modern dwelling. The design centers around a new courtyard on the first floor within the walls of the existing building with a glazed gable end that opens up to become part of the main living space. Original stone walls were restored with a highly insulated timber box inserted inside them. The roof, built from timber salvaged from the building, was engineered without ties so that the space can be used. Old on the outside, new on the inside, the house is a surprise – quite different from what its exterior indicates. It is the perfect place to start exploring its beautiful locality.

View of the living room. Interior courtyard.
The original stone façade from the street. Interior
view of the kitchen.

One of the bedrooms with modern design. Detail of
the metal stair. The children's bedroom. Cross section.

GETTING AROUND. THIS PART OF
DEVON IS HOME TO SOME OF
ENGLAND'S MOST BEAUTIFUL
BEACHES. BANTHAM, THE AREA'S
BEST SURFING AND KITE SURFING
BEACH, IS ONLY A 10-MINUTE DRIVE
AWAY AND THERE ARE DOZENS
OF AMAZING BEACHES FROM
MOTHECOME AND BIGBURY TO
THE SOUTH TO SLAPTON AND
BLACKPOOL SANDS TOWARDS
DARTMOUTH. MANY OF THEM ARE
CONNECTED BY COASTAL PATHS
THAT OFFER SPECTACULAR WALKING.

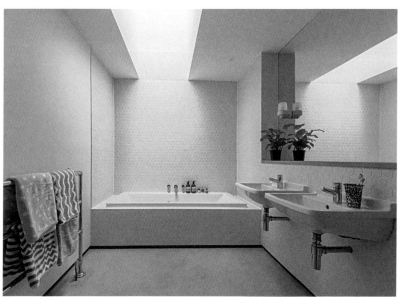

View of the kitchen open to courtyard.
Bright bathroom with skylight.

Main view from the garden. Detail of the corridor with wood furniture. The house nestled in the surrounding nature. Dining and living area with fireplace.

Ferienhaus am früheren Seilerhansenhof

FURTWANGEN, GERMANY

Incorporating the generous proportions and open nature of the valley were key considerations for the design. The wish for protected outdoor spaces was met with a three-part concept. This resulted in a cluster of three building parts, which then again combine to create various outdoor spaces. The agricultural setting was another determining factor. A sequence of gabled roofs matches the hills and topography of the landscape. The architectural vocabulary conveys a down-to-earth clarity that is visibly reflected and discernible in the ensemble. The design is based on clear and simple premises.

The window placement reveals what is going on inside – room sequences, views, gradations that combine into a mostly open residential environment.

All windows are derived from the interior layout of the houses and follow a functional logic too, create deliberate views, atmospheres and specific spaces. This interplay of compact closed building structures and surprising interior spaces determines the architecture. All rooms offer views of open nature. A small brook, the Schützenbach, meanders around the building.

INFORMATION. ARCHITECTS>
KUBERCZYK ARCHITEKTUR,
CHRISTIAN KUBERCZYK ARCHITEKT //
2017. HOUSE> 4 GUESTS //
2 BEDROOMS // 1 BATHROOM.
ADDRESS> VORDERSCHÜTZENBACH,
FURTWANGEN, GERMANY.
WWW.SEILERHANSENHOF.DE

GETTING AROUND. STARTING FROM THE LOCATION AND THE SURROUNDING MAGNIFICENT NATURE, GUESTS CAN HIKE, BIKE, MOUNTAIN BIKE, SKI; VISIT THE FELDBERG MOUNTAIN, AS WELL AS THE CITY OF FREIBURG AND THE ALSACE REGION. AN ARCHITECTURAL HIGHLIGHT IN THE VICINITY IS THE LANDMARKED LINACH DAM, GERMANY'S ONLY MULTIPLE ARCHED DAM.

General view of the house. Floor plan.
View of the outdoor terrace.

One of the bedrooms. The dining room
from above. View of the house from the garden.

INFORMATION. ARCHITECT>
HEIKE WITTENBECHER // 2016.
WASSERTURM> 80 SQM // 2 GUESTS //
1 BEDROOM // 1 BATHROOM.
ADDRESS> BAD SAAROW, GERMANY.
WWW.WASSERTURM-BADSAAROW.DE
WWW.WASSERWERK-BADSAAROW.DE

*View of the bedroom from above. Night view of the
lighthouse. Great view from the roof terrace, with
glass wall and bubble chairs.*

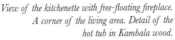

View of the kitchenette with free-floating fireplace.
A corner of the living area. Detail of the
hot tub in Kambala wood.

Wasserturm
Bad Saarow

BAD SAAROW, GERMANY

Built more than 100 years ago on the shore of Scharmützelsee lake, millions of liters of water have passed through it and Max Schmeling and Maxim Gorki walked past it on the way to their homes. Then it was abandoned for a long time, its water tank removed, and left to decay. Now it has been given a second life. Its all-round glazed extension offers a fantastic view of possibly Germany's most beautiful lake, the thermal spa and spa park, and the forests of Brandenburg.

Visitors can now forget about the world for a while seated in front of the free-standing fireplace or relaxing in the whirlpool made of Kambala wood. The old water tower invites everyone to relax, dream, and take it easy.

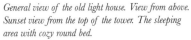
General view of the old light house. View from above.
Sunset view from the top of the tower. The sleeping
area with cozy round bed.

GETTING AROUND. GUESTS CAN
WALK IN BATHROBES TO GERMANY'S
MOST BEAUTIFUL THERMAL SPA AND
THANKS TO THE GOOD NEIGHBORLY
RELATIONS ENJOY SPECIAL OFFERS
SUCH AS A "MUD PACK IN THE
MOONSHINE" OR A "ROMANTIC
NIGHT". THOSE WHO FIND THE
WATER OF THE WHIRLPOOL AND SPA
TOO HOT CAN WALK A FEW METERS
THROUGH THE SPA GARDEN TO
JUMP INTO THE CLEAR WATER OF
THE SCHARMÜTZELSEE. ON A
NEIGHBORING LAKE, BEGINNERS
AND EXPERTS CAN PRACTICE
THEIR WAKEBOARDING SKILLS.
THE ODER-SPREE BICYCLE PATH
PASSES IMMEDIATELY NEXT TO
THE WATER TOWER.

INFORMATION. ARCHITECTS>
PEDEVILLA ARCHITECTS // 2017.
HOTEL> 30–45 SQM EACH ROOM //
80–90 GUESTS // 44 BEDROOMS //
44 BATHROOMS.
ADDRESS> AM BÜHEL, ST. JAKOB
IM AHRNTAL, SOUTH TYROL, ITALY.
WWW.BUEHELWIRT.COM

*View of the larch wood furniture. Private bedroom
with panoramic view. Exterior view of the new
geometric form of the added building. Main view of
the building.*

Hotel Bühelwirt

SOUTH TYROL, ITALY

The venerable hikers' hotel is located on the "Bühel", directly next to the village church at a height of 1,200 meters above sea level. In order not to limit the use, views, and sunlight exposure of the existing structure, the extension was positioned towards the valley to the north. The new building with 20 rooms, restaurant and wellness area extends across six floors and derives its unique shape from an asymmetrical gabled roof and laterally protruding oriels, which respond to the local climate.

The green luster of the black timber façade reflects the hues of the satiated green to deep black forests. As a result, nature and topography seem to blend into the building. The rooms are reduced to the bare minimum with a focus on the view of the mountains. Characteristic elements of the local building style were adopted and reinterpreted. The larch wood from the surrounding forests conveys a cozy feeling. The green luster of the plaster surfaces containing aggregates from the nearby copper mine reflect the color schemes of the mountains and adds a familiar touch to the interior.

At the same time, the lamps that are manually enhanced with copper and the curtains made by the local loden cloth manufacturer create a powerful regional association.

Side view of the building, nestled in the surrounding landscape. One of the private rooms.

View from the balcony of the green forest.
Detail of the black wooden façade. Interior view.
Side view.

GETTING AROUND. THE BÜHELWIRT IS A CENTRAL STARTING POINT FOR A VARIETY OF HIKING AND MOUNTAIN BIKE TOURS IN THE REGION. DARING GUESTS TEST THE MODERN HIGH ROPE COURSE OR VENTURE ON A RAFTING TRIP. THE AHRNTAL IS AN INSIDER TIP FOR SNOWSHOEING AND SNOW TOURS; IT IS A WINTER WONDERLAND FOR FAMILIES WITH TOBOGGANS OR SKIS. THE MINING MUSEUM PRETTAU, THE IMPRESSIVE TAUFERS FORTRESS, OR THE MESSNER MOUNTAIN MUSEUM ARE CULTURAL ATTRACTIONS IN THE VICINITY.

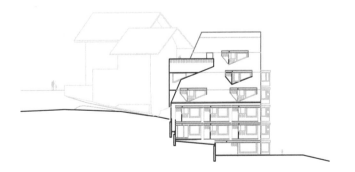

161

INFORMATION. ARCHITECTS>
2001 JOSÉ LUIS FORTEZA ARTIGUES,
2017 AND FOLLOWING: BETTINA
MACHEL AND SKA HAMBURG.
VILLA> 415 SQM // 10 GUESTS //
4 BEDROOMS // 4 BATHROOMS.
ADDRESS> FELANITX, MAJORCA,
SPAIN.
WWW.FINCA-CAN-CIREROL.COM

*View of the bright living room. Detail of stairs and
work area. Panoramic view from the pool. Main view
of the finca from the garden.*

Finca Can Cirerol

MAJORCA, SPAIN

The finca Can Cirerol is located on an elevation above Porto Colom, only 1.9 kilometers from the port. Majorca's largest natural harbor, Porto Colom is a fishing village that is preserved in its original state, where tourists can still meet the local inhabitants. Legend has it that the seafarer Christopher Columbus was born here. The finca Can Cirerol also bridges the gap between tradition and modernity. Similar to the southeast of Majorca, which has not been flooded by tourists, the finca offers on the one hand much room for the leisure and regeneration of individual guests, coupled with the opportunity of everyone interacting in a relaxed atmosphere in the sun. The second generation of owners is very keen on bringing all newly created elements in the house and garden in harmony with the local building tradition and nature. They are less interested in cool, replaceable design, but rather in the shadow of a "coming home" atmosphere.

View of the house from the pool.
The garden with outdoor kitchen.

Interior view of one of the bedrooms. Exterior lounge space. View from the dining room. Ground floor plan.

GETTING AROUND. THE FINCA CAN CIREROL IS ONLY A FEW MINUTES AWAY FROM THE ENCHANTING TOWN OF PORTO COLOM. THE IDYLLIC FISHING HARBOR WELCOMES ITS GUESTS WITH A LARGE NATURAL BAY. SMALL RESTAURANTS ON THE HARBOR PROMENADE ARE AS INVITING AS THE CASUAL BEACH BARS WITH A FANTASTIC VIEW OF THE SUNSET ON THE EASTERN SHORE OF THE BAY.

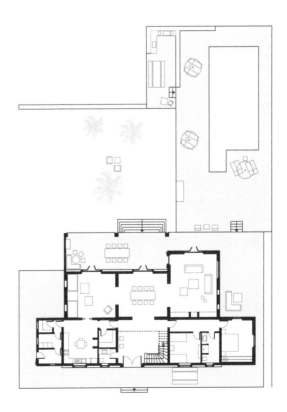

INFORMATION. ARCHITECTS> OFFICE KERSTEN GEERS AND DAVID VAN SEVEREN – PART OF THE SOLO HOUSES PROJECT DEVELOPED BY CHRISTIAN BOURDAIS // 2017. HOUSE> 452 SQM // 2–8 GUESTS // ADDRESS> MATARRAÑA, SPAIN. WWW.SOLO-HOUSES.COM

Exterior view of the house.
View from the garden.
View from inside the bedroom.

Solo Office

MATARRAÑA, SPAIN

Belgian architects Office Kersten Geers and David Van Severen created the second house of the Solo Houses collection, after the Chilean duo Pezo Von Ellrichshausen. Located on a natural plateau that offers an incredible 360-degree panorama, its design questions the very definition of a house.

Although Solo Office incorporated all the usual structural elements: concrete foundations, a mobile façade that contains the three housing units, a flat roof supported by four rows of nine columns, and a set of furniture, it is a unique object that defies all conventions. The total area of 1,600 square meters including a patio of 1,050 square meters with a swimming pool, master bedroom and guest room, measuring 60 square meters each, is simultaneously discreet and imposing, ceremonial and sparse, open and introverted, transparent and opaque, luxurious and austere. According to the architects, the Solo House II is an exercise in the manufacture of an architecture that is not just a result of a single system. Its systems were designed and reinvented by others, such as the outdoor modules of the house by artist Pieter Vermeersch, the lamps-stools hybrid by artist Richard Venlet, or the iconic line of furniture by Muller Van Severen (wireS). Hedonists will undoubtedly admire this project for the idea of low resolution at its best, which is probably the most outstanding feature of this unique and exceptional construction.

GETTING AROUND. THE REGION WHERE THE SOLO OFFICE IS LOCATED OFFERS MANY OUTDOOR ACTIVITIES AS WELL AS VISITS TO NEARBY MEDIEVAL VILLAGES. IN WARM WEATHER GUESTS CAN ALSO ENJOY THE BEACHES OF THE EBRO DELTA NATURE RESERVE.

Outdoor area and entrance. View of the bedroom.
Exterior view from below.

Kitchen with panorama view.
View of the studio. Exterior view.

INFORMATION. ARCHITECTS>
MARGOT + EDWARD JONES // 2003.
HOUSE> 250 SQM // 8 GUESTS //
4 BEDROOMS // 5 BATHROOMS.
ADDRESS> LES ADRETS, BARGEMON,
FRANCE.
WWW.VILLAJONES.COM

Villa Jones

BARGEMON, FRANCE

The first occupancy of the site was a small shepherd's hut with a magnificent view south through the hills towards the Mediterranean. The design of the house is directly related to the conditions of the site with its topography of stepped terraces formed by dry stonewalls, which had been used for the cultivation of olives 2,000 years ago. An early inspiration was the Italian villa/garden tradition, in which the slope of the land intersects with the precise terraces and the disciplined contours encourage ideas of linearity. Pergola, loggia, court, and lawn extend the boundaries of the house into a comprehensive composition. The sequence of the living room, double height loggia, kitchen/ dining room and swimming pool court are all connected enfilade. To the south of these spaces a 60-meter-long pergola frames the garden and the view. The house is long in plan but narrow in section, open to the south and closed to the north and giving all rooms the benefit of the view. Le Corbusier declared that a house should be a "machine à habiter". This aphorism might be extended here, whereby the house acts as a mechanism for viewing the landscape with some views accidental and others planned.

View of the dining room. Exterior view of the house from the pool. The villa nestled in the surrounding nature. View from the garden.

View of the bedroom. Detail of the pergola in the garden. Floor plans. View of the covered terrace with large fireplace.

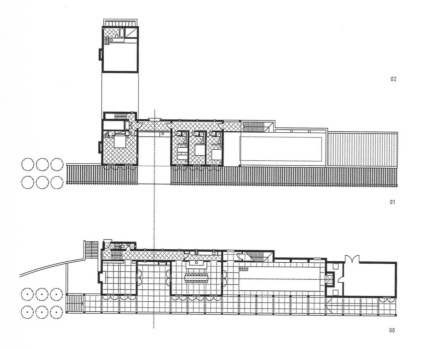

02

01

00

GETTING AROUND. THE SITE IS LOCATED 2 KILOMETERS NORTH-EAST OF THE TOWN OF BARGEMON PROVENCE AND ONE HOUR FROM NICE. THE COL DU BEL HOMME, IMME-DIATELY BEHIND, FORMS A NATURAL BARRIER TO THE NORTH AND MARKS THE LIMIT OF HABITATION BEFORE THE COMMENCEMENT OF THE MILITARY ZONE. THE RELATIONSHIP BETWEEN THE HOUSE AND GARDEN IS FASCINATING, PARTICULARLY IN THE MEDITERRANEAN CLIMATE WHERE THE RELATIONSHIP BETWEEN INSIDE AND OUTSIDE IS ALWAYS AMBIGUOUS.

INFORMATION. ARCHITECTS>
GIORGIO GULLOTTA ARCHITEKTEN
// 2016. HOUSE> 35 GUESTS //
13 BEDROOMS // 13 BATHROOMS.
ADDRESS> SCHULTERBLATT,
HAMBURG, GERMANY.
WWW.AUGUSTBOARDINGHOUSE.COM

One of the fully equipped kitchens.
View of one of the bathrooms.

August the Boardinghouse

HAMBURG, GERMANY

With a loving touch and a keen sense of art and design these lodgings cater to the needs of real big city lovers. The fully renovated apartments are equipped with everything modern-day nomads require to feel at home.

The boardinghouse August with its green idyllic backyard offers guests a retreat right in the heart of Hamburg. Whether for a short or long stay, alone or with many others, everyone is always welcome to kick off their shoes and enjoy their stay. The guests are made to feel comfortable and at home.

They are encouraged to behave as if they were in their own homes. Furnished with individual works of art and Scandinavian design furniture, the apartments feature satellite TVs in the bedrooms and free Wi-Fi. Luxury box spring beds ensure comfortable sleep in the home-like setting.

View of the living room with scandinavian design furniture. Detail of the sleeping room.

GETTING AROUND. YOU CAN FEEL THE URBAN PULSE OF THE CITY RIGHT OUTSIDE THE FRONT DOOR. THE SCHANZEN URBAN DISTRICT ATTRACTS ARTISTS, GALLERY OWNERS AND OTHER CREATIVE INDIVIDUALS AT ALL TIMES DAY AND NIGHT. THE RESULT IS A COLORFUL MIX OF FRENCH CUISINE, ORIENTAL TAKEAWAY AND FRESH PRODUCE ON THE FARMERS' MARKET. THE PATCHWORK-STYLE OFFER OF DINING AND CULTURE LENDS MUCH TO DISCOVER AND IT IS UP TO YOU AND YOUR INDIVIDUAL GOOD TASTE TO SELECT YOUR FAVORITES. YOU CAN ALSO REACH THE ALSTER OR ELBE RIVERS BY FOOT, BY BICYCLE, OR BY PUBLIC TRANSPORTATION.

View of the bedroom. Private balcony with garden view. Details of the dining area.

View of the living room. Detail of the Scandinavian design furniture. View of the kitchen.

INFORMATION. ARCHITECTS>
FRANCESCO DI GREGORIO &
KARIN MATZ // 2012. HOUSE>
85 SQM // 5 GUESTS //
3 BEDROOMS // 1 BATHROOM.
ADDRESS> ALKERSUM, FÖHR,
GERMANY.
WWW.FRANCESCODIGREGORIO.IT
WWW.KARINMATZ.SE

Föhr House

FÖHR, GERMANY

The project is located on Föhr, a small island in the North Sea. In the village of Alkersum, the former hay storage of a traditional farmhouse was redefined by a timber structure covered by 3,200 tiles, each with a handmade circular hole, 500 meters of polypropylene blue rope, and treated pine wood. The architects lived in the house on the island while the renovation was carried out during three autumn months. Together with the owner they carried out some of the tasks themselves like drilling holes in the 3,200 tiles one tile at a time, and the construction of the rope around the staircase, the lighting of the rooms, and other small details. The space was reopened by taking down all dividing walls except for the ones surrounding the bathroom. A new volume was added, which became the central wall going through and unifying the space. It is covered in ceramic tiles with a simple pattern provided by the blue cement holding them. Light is introduced by the reflective ceramics and the translucent doors. Threads frame the staircase, creating a transparent threshold. Sometimes, one only recognizes the outcome of creative work after it is done. The architects returned in the summer and realized what they had built – a stranded ship.

View of the dining room. Main view of the house.
Detail of the natural pool. Interior view.

View of one of the bedrooms and the private living room. Interior view of the house. Floor plan. Detail of the modern stairs.

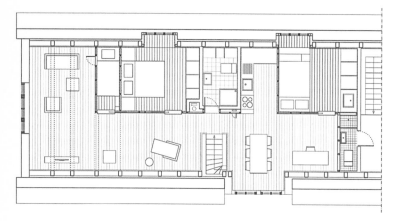

GETTING AROUND. DUE TO ITS GEOGRAPHICAL LOCATION, FÖHR IS VERY MUCH IN THE HANDS OF NATURAL FORCES AND HAS A POWERFUL TIDE. IN SUMMER THE POPULATION INCREASES FROM 8,500 TO 40,000 DUE TO TOURISM. THE ISLAND BELONGS TO GERMANY BUT FIRST AND FOREMOST TO THE NORTH FRISIA REGION. THE FRISIANS HAVE THEIR OWN LANGUAGE AND CULTURE. TYPICAL ARE FRISIAN TILES AND WOOD PAINTED IN NUANCES OF BLUE-GREEN, BRICK HOUSES WITH THATCHED ROOFS, AND BED-BOXES.

INFORMATION. ARCHITECT> CARLA GERTZ // 2017. CABIN> 115 SQM // 4 GUESTS // 2 BEDROOMS // 1 BATHROOM. ADDRESS> SAVITAIPALE, FINLAND. WWW.CGERTZ.JIMDO.COM

Mökki Santara

SAVITAIPALE, FINLAND

The Finnish term "Mökki" describes a small cottage by the lake – a quiet retreat, surrounded only by nature. Without luxury, reduced to the essential, the Mökki traditionally links urban everyday life to proximity with nature. It is a peaceful place, embedded in the heart of Karelia amidst the endless wilderness of forests and lakes. Following traditional spatial concepts, the Mökki divides the functions of living and cleaning into two separate volumes. Slightly elevated on a connecting platform, these volumes open to southwest, overlooking Lake Santara. The simple, archetypal buildings offer a unique and contemporary interpretation of the Mökki typology. When closed, the volumes look like black, archaic monoliths. The interior

contrasts with the exterior appearance with a light and warm flowing sequence of rooms. White and untreated wooden surfaces divide the kitchen, living and sleeping area into different zones. The exclusive use of regional and sustainable materials emphasizes the site-specific approach. The spruce timber for the Mökki was sourced and dried on location and now provides a comforting atmosphere, even when it is -30° C outside. Prefabrication of the supporting construction elements as well as the windows, doors and built-in furniture made it possible to complete the construction of the Mökki Santara in only 8 weeks. The result of this careful yet somehow natural approach to design and construction is a gentle architecture for a quiet setting.

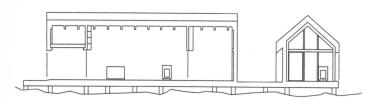

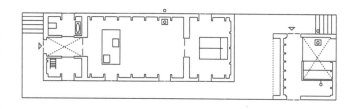

GETTING AROUND. "THE FINNISH AFFINITY WITH NATURE DEMANDS A COUNTERBALANCE TO THE EVERYDAY APARTMENT: THE SUMMER COTTAGE OR MÖKKI. IT IS QUITE TRUE TO SAY THE FINNISH PEOPLE LIVE THEIR REAL LIFE IN THEIR COTTAGE". - TAPIO PERIÄINEN, DIRECTOR OF THE FINNISH SOCIETY OF CRAFTS AND DESIGN.

The cabin nestled in the snowy landscape. Cross section and floor plan. View from the living room. General view.

INFORMATION. ARCHITECTS>
OFIS ARCHITECTS // 2016.
CABIN> 9.7 SQM // 9 GUESTS.
ADDRESS> MOUNT KANIN, SLOVENIA.
WWW.PZS.SI

Winter Cabin on Mount Kanin

MOUNT KANIN, SLOVENIA

The aim of this project was to install real objects, i.e. 1:1 shelters, at remote sites and study their response to extreme weather, radical temperature shifts, snow, landslides, and rugged terrain, all of which require specific architectural forms, structures and concepts. The site is accessible only by climbing or helicopter – thus the modules and loads were prepared according to the maximum weight and equilibrium limits. Its position within the wilderness requires respect of natural resources to ensure the stability of the shelter with minimum impact on the ground. Kanin Winter Cabin forms a compact wooden volume organized of three floor platforms that are suspended towards the valley with a large glazed panoramic window offering astonishing views. A cantilevered overhang, the resting part of the cabin, creates the smallest footprint on the rock. The interior is modest, subordinate to the function, and provides accommodation for up to nine mountaineers.

The cabin placement and transportation was extremely difficult carried out by the Slovene Armed Forces helicopter crew. Bad weather and unexpected turbulences led to the cabin being placed and fixed on site at the third attempt. However, the challenge of the project is to gain new knowledge through unexpected weather conditions. Winter Cabin has been fully implemented with donations and many hard working volunteer hours.

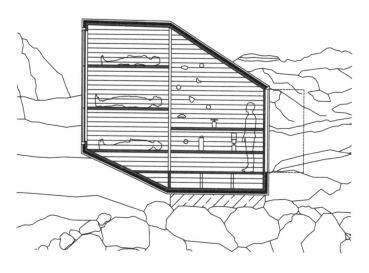

GETTING AROUND. KANIN IS A MOUNTAIN ABOVE THE SMALL TOWN OF BOVEC, WITH BEAUTIFUL RESORTS NEARBY. THE AREA IS ALSO RENOWNED FOR BATTLES THAT TOOK PLACE DURING THE WORLD WAR WITH MANY REMAINS STILL FOUND IN THE AREA. THIS PARTICULAR SITE WAS CHOSEN BECAUSE OF ITS 360-DEGREE VIEWS OVER SLOVENIA AND ITALY, AND SPECTACULAR VIEWS TO TRIGLAV, SOCA VALLEY AND ADRIATIC SEA. IT IS A DESTINATION FOR HIKERS, CLIMBERS, CAVERS, MOUNTAINEERS, NATURE LOVERS AND ROMANTICS.

Main view from below. Cross section. Back view of the Winter Cabin surrounded by the mountains.

Interior view. Detail of the large panoramic window. Exterior side view.

7132 Hotel

VALS, SWITZERLAND

*Main view of the hotel surrounded by the Vals Valley.
Interior view of the bedroom "Stone" designed by
Thom Mayne. Terrace with fireplace.*

The 7132 Hotel is located in the picturesque village of Vals in the Grison Alps of Switzerland, with an idyllic landscape, archaic mountains and much room for innovation. With its famous thermal spring, Vals is a quiet spa retreat and guests can enjoy its very special atmosphere at the 7132 Hotel. They can escape the uninspired mainstream and experience the last true luxury of our hectic times: leisure, quiet and deceleration at an inspiring stylish location for relaxation, pampering and enjoying the moment. 7132 offers all that with an exceptional architecture, noble design, exquisite cuisine and an internationally famous thermal spa. The latest renovation phase was completed in July 2017. In addition to a number of new rooms, the reception and lobby were redecorated along with the bar and the garden featuring a pavilion and relaxation terraces. A large library with an open fireplace was also added. To support the year-round use of the premises, four high-quality meeting rooms were added with room for up to 40 persons each.

The unique characteristic of Vals was also the basis for the hotel's name. 7132 is the postal code of the community and became the trademark for a new tourism concept with the declared goals of shunning mass tourism and preserving the original nature and exclusivity of the offerings in Vals. All activities of the company are operated under this name, or rather this number.

INFORMATION. ARCHITECTS>
PETER ZUMTHOR, KENGO KUMA,
TADAO ANDO AND THOM MAYNE //
2017. HOTEL> 190 GUESTS // HOUSE
OF ARCHITECTS> 20 SQM EACH
ROOM // 23 KUMA ROOMS,
22 MAYNE ROOMS, 18 ANDO ROOMS,
10 ZUMTHOR ROOMS // HOTEL
SUPERIOR> 3 PENTHOUSE SUITES,
3 SPA SUITES, 12 SPA DELUXE ROOMS,
3 DOUBLE ROOMS, 1 SINGLE ROOM.
ADDRESS> VALS, SWITZERLAND.
WWW.7132.COM

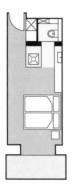  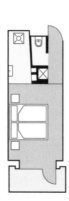 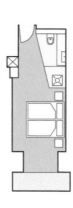

GETTING AROUND. VALS IS UNIQUELY DISTINGUISHED BY ITS LEGENDARY THERMAL SPRING. THE HIGHLY MINERALIZED WATER THAT GUSHES FORTH FROM IT AT A TEMPERATURE OF 30 °C HAS BEEN ATTRACTING VISITORS FOR MORE THAN 100 YEARS. ARCHITECT PETER ZUMTHOR BECAME FAMOUS IN 1996 WITH HIS DESIGN FOR A NEW BATHING FACILITY. THE MONOLITHIC BUILDING MADE OF RAW CONCRETE AND 60,000 VALS QUARTZITE BLOCKS PAYS HOMAGE TO THE ARCHAIC BEAUTY OF THE VALS VALLEY.

View of the room designed by Kengo Kuma like an oak cocoon. Floor plans. View of the valley from the bedroom.

The room designed by Peter Zumthor with classical atmosphere. Japanese details for the bedroom designed by Tadao Ando. View of the spa suite.

INFORMATION. ARCHITECTS> UMMO STUDIO // DESIGNER AND ARTIST> PILAR DEL PINO LÓPEZ // 2012. CAVE HOUSE> 104 SQM // 2–4 GUESTS // 1 BEDROOM // 1 BATHROOM. ADDRESS> FARM CUEVAS DEL PINO, CÓRDOBA , SPAIN. WWW.CUEVASDELPINO.COM

View of the open space. Details of the furniture. Interior view. Main view of the cave house from the garden.

Casa Tierra

CÓRDOBA , SPAIN

Casa Tierra (Earth House), a unique troglodyte dwelling from the 21st century is located at Cuevas del Pino farm, 15 minutes from Córdoba, Spain. The estate sits in the foothills of Sierra Morena, in a calcarenite rock terrain. During the 19th and 20th century the area was used for farming, and even featured a bullring in which the most important bullfighters of the time competed in 2009.

Today the site has been converted into rural housing and accommodates new countryside activities. Both the preexisting walls and the rock itself defined an area of great spatial and material wealth. For this reason, the intervention focused on a continuous dialogue between the preexisting conditions and the new

architecture: clean and quiet volumes, bright spaces, hard materials, such as concrete and glass, openings to conjure natural light, and handcrafted wooden furniture to give warmth to the cave house.

This house stands inside the open-air stone quarry. It is accessed through the enchanting 3,000-square-meter garden. Guests can relax here in an almost subterranean silence, while contemplating the sky and trees through the window. The temperature stays at a constant 18 to 20 °C all year round. This is a gift during the very hot Cordovan summers, while at the same time ensuring cozy and warm winters.

View of the kitchen. Night view. Detail of the bathroom. Cross section.

GETTING AROUND. THE OWNERS ORGANIZE EVENTS RELATED TO NATURE AND ART, E.G. THE FESTIVAL OF PATIOS. THE HOUSE IS WELL SITUATED FOR VISITING ANY PROVINCE OF ANDALUSIA AND ONLY 7 KILOMETERS FROM THE MEDINA AZAHARA RUINS OF CALIPH CITY. GUESTS CAN STOP ON THE WAY AT MONTILLA VILLAGES, WHERE THE LOCAL FINO WINE ORIGINATES. OR THEY CAN GET A CANOE AND ROW DOWN THE RIVER GUADALQUIVIER. AT NIGHT THEY CAN ADMIRE THE BILLIONS OF STARS.

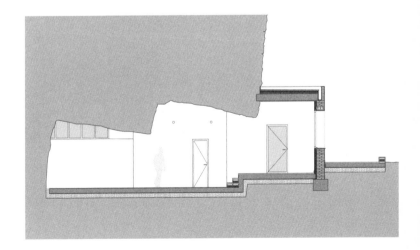

INFORMATION. ARCHITECTS>
JEANNA BERGER, JONAS FRED HELL
AND ROBERT FRIDH // 2017.
CABIN> 5 SQM // 2 GUESTS //
1 BEDROOM. ADDRESS>
HENRIKSHOLM, DALSLAND, SWEDEN.
WWW.72HCABIN.COM

The cabin nestled in the surrounding nature.
Details of the bed. Exterior back view.
Main view of the cabin.

The 72 Hour Cabin

HENRIKSHOLM, DALSLAND, SWEDEN

In autumn 2017, five people with stressful jobs were given the chance to try the Swedish "close to nature" lifestyle and find a new perspective on life at a 72-hours' stay, set in the natural surroundings of Dalsland. Given Dalsland's natural wonders, it provides the perfect setting for the 72 Hour Cabin wellbeing project. An initiative of Visit Sweden and the West Sweden Tourist Board, the project aimed at measuring the effect of a stay in Dalsland on the wellbeing of five individuals, all of who lead stressful lives. Each participant moved into a glass house on an island in Dalsland and participated in a number of activities including making a fire in the open, canoeing and activities that average Swedes normally enjoy while on vacation. At night,

the participants were able to enjoy the star-filled, clear skies through the glass ceilings of their rooms. Researchers from the renowned Karolinska Institute in Stockholm tracked the wellbeing of the participants. The results were positive and now everyone can enjoy the feeling of wellbeing in Dalsland's natural surroundings.

The five original cabins are beautifully located on privately owned Henriksholm island in southeast Dalsland. Henriksholm is like a miniature Sweden. When you book this unique stay, on arrival you will be given tips on the wonderful local hiking trails, a fishing rod, and access to rowing boats.

Main view from the water. View from below.
Sunset view from the bed. View of the glass roof from
above.

GETTING AROUND. THE NATURE
OF DALSLAND IN WEST SWEDEN IS
GRAND, WILD AND BEAUTIFUL. WITH
ITS DEEP FORESTS, WATERFALLS,
VERDANT PLANS AND MYRIAD LAKES,
THERE ARE INFINITE OPPORTUNITIES
FOR NATURE EXPERIENCES. YOU
CAN COME FOR THE HIKING TRIPS, CY-
CLING, PADDLING, CLIMBING, HORSE
RIDING, FISHING AND FORAGING. OR
JUST RELAX. DALSLAND IS A PLACE
THAT APPEALS TO ALL THE SENSES.

Map of Europe

- ⊙ CITIES AND METROPOLISES
- ⊙ MOUNTAINS AND COUNTRYSIDE
- ⊙ SEA AND LAKES

Places to go and things to do

an index of accommodations and activities

 CLIMBING

 CYCLING

RESTAURANTS

GOLF

HIKING

KAYAKING

SIGHTSEEING

SAILING

SHOPPING

RIDING

SKIING

SWIMMING

WINE TASTING

 CITIES AND
METROPOLISES

**AUGUST THE BOARDINGHOUSE /
GERMANY**
WWW.AUGUSTBOARDINGHOUSE.COM
   174

CASA DO ROSÁRIO / PORTUGAL
WWW.AIRBNB.DE/ROOMS/11132494
   50

**HAFENCITY HAFENKRAN /
GERMANY**
WWW.FLOATEL.DE
    58

PORT X / CZECH REPUBLIC
WWW.PORTX.CZ
   46

VIPP LOFT / DENMARK
WWW.VIPP.COM/HOTEL
   106

 MOUNTAINS AND
COUNTRYSIDE

7132 HOTEL / SWITZERLAND
WWW.7132.COM
   190

**ATELIER LACHAERT DHANIS /
BELGIUM**
WWW.ATELIERLACHAERTDHANIS.COM
   118

**BASSIVIÈRE BARN CHIC /
FRANCE**
WWW.BASSIVIERE.COM
     90

BOXWOOD / ENGLAND
WWW.BOXWOOD-RETREAT.CO.UK
    134

CASA DA RAMPA / PORTUGAL
WWW.BOUTIQUE-HOMES.COM/
VACATION-RENTALS/EUROPE/
PORTUGAL/CASA-DA-RAMPA-
SINTRA-PORTUGAL
   62

CASA TIERRA / SPAIN
WWW.CUEVASDELPINO.COM
194

 SEA AND LAKES

BACKWATER / ENGLAND
WWW.BACKWATERNORFOLK.CO.UK
 54

BREAC HOUSE / IRELAND
WWW.BREAC.HOUSE
 18

BUDE BARN / ENGLAND
WWW.VENN-FARM.CO.UK
 102

CASA AGOSTOS / PORTUGAL
WWW.FACEBOOK.COM/
CASAAGOSTOS
 30

CASA MODESTA / PORTUGAL
WWW.CASAMODESTA.PT
 14

CASA XYZA / PORTUGAL
WWW.CASAXYZA.COM
 74

DEZANOVE HOUSE / SPAIN
WWW.DEZANOVEHOUSE.COM
 98

FINCA CAN CIREROL / SPAIN
WWW.FINCA-CAN-CIREROL.COM
 162

FÖHR HOUSE / GERMANY
WWW.FRANCESCODIGREGORIO.IT
WWW.KARINMATZ.SE
 178

HOLIDAY APARTMENT IN MIĘDZYZDROJE / POLAND
WWW.LOFT-KOLASINSKI.COM
 38

KUĆA FOTOGRAFA / CROATIA
WWW.KUCAFOTOGRAFA.COM
 26

LANDHAUS FERGITZ / GERMANY
WWW.LANDHAUS-FERGITZ.COM
 130

MÖKKI SANTARA / FINLAND
WWW.CGERTZ.JIMDO.COM
 182

NEWHAUS / GERMANY
WWW.NEWHAUS.DE
 142

ÖÖD / ESTONIA
WWW.OODHOUSE.COM
 10

THE 72 HOUR CABIN / SWEDEN
WWW.72HCABIN.COM
 198

THE MALTHOUSE / ENGLAND
WWW.MALTHOU.SE
 146

TINHOUSE / SCOTLAND
WWW.TINHOUSE.NET
34

TREEHOUSE SPOT / PORTUGAL
WWW.VISITSETUBAL.COM.PT/EN/
HOTEIS/ECOPARQUE-DO-OUTAO
70

WASSERTURM BAD SAAROW / GERMANY
WWW.WASSERTURM-BADSAAROW.DE
WWW.WASSERWERK-BADSAAROW.DE
 154

Picture
Credits

All other pictures were made available
by the architects, designers, or hosts.

Cover front: Jonas Ingman
Cover back (from left to right,
from above to below): Belen Imaz,
Bas Princen, Tiberio Sorvillo,
Michael Kromat